the WORD of PROMISE next generation

devotional & journal

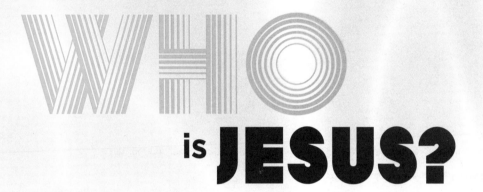

WHO is JESUS?

THOMAS NELSON
Since 1798

NASHVILLE   DALLAS   MEXICO CITY   RIO DE JANEIRO   BEIJING

WHO Is Jesus, a WORD of PROMISE next generation® Devotional and Journal

Copyright © 2009 by Thomas Nelson, Inc.

Who Is Jesus was written by Brenda Noel, co-producer, writer and production supervisor of *The Word of Promise Next Generation*.

Audio selections taken from *The Word of Promise, Next Generation*®
PRODUCED BY CARL AMARI
MUSIC BY ROB POTTORF
DIRECTED BY JOHN KIRBY

Bible text selections from the *Reader Friendly Edition*™, formerly titled the *International Children's Bible*®
Copyright © 1986, 1988, 1999 by Thomas Nelson, Inc.

Design and Cover by Jade Novak

Interior page layout and typeset by Koechel Peterson and Associates, Minneapolis, MN

ISBN 9781400315581

Printed in the USA

RRD
Crawfordsville, IN/US
October 2009
PO #96807

1 2 3 4 5 – 13 12 11 10 09

TABLE OF CONTENTS

de·fine[*it*]

DEFINE IT: This section allows you to explore words you may not know about, find their meanings, and learn about their importance in the Bible and your life.

INTRODUCTION

Jesus.

OK, you hear about Him at church, at Easter time, at Christmas time. You are told about how much He loves you. You may know that you should believe in Him and love Him.

But who is He? What makes this particular man so different?

The best way to find the answer to that question is to listen to the things that the Bible says about Him and the things He said about Himself.

Centuries before Jesus was born, God told the prophets (people who could hear God's voice) that He would send a very special man to earth. This man would be His Son.

With God as His Father and a human woman as His mother, this man would be completely God and completely man. (Think of light. It's completely clear, but really, it is every color combined. That's why when light shines through water drops, it makes a rainbow. So light is clear *and* color at the same time.)

de·fine[it]

ANOINTED This word means to pour or rub oil on something or someone. When something is anointed it is set apart or chosen for special service to God.

God called this man the Messiah, which means "anointed one." The promised Messiah would be God's Son and would reveal God's love and truth to people and show them how to become part of God's kingdom.

Hundreds of years after God first promised to send His Son, God sent an angel to a young woman named Mary. Although Mary had never been with a man, the angel told her that she was soon to give birth to a child. Through the power of the Holy Spirit, God Himself would be the baby's Father! Being both God and man, this baby would be the long awaited Messiah. The angel told her to name this miraculous baby Jesus.

As a child, Jesus lived with His mother and her husband, Joseph, who was a carpenter. Jesus most likely spent many hours working at Joseph's side and learning how to fashion things from wood.

To everyone who knew Him, Jesus must have seemed very ordinary. But there was one huge difference with Jesus—He *never* sinned! He always acted with love and consideration of others. He always did only the things that pleased His Father. Can you imagine what a wonderful Son and friend He was?

After Joseph died, Jesus stayed with His mother and cared for her by working as a carpenter. Because Jesus was a man as well as God, He grew up just like we do and

He went through a lot of the same things that we do. Jesus felt pain, sadness, love, and disappointment. He probably skinned His knees as a boy and hit His thumb with the hammer a few times.

But He was more than a carpenter, and, at the age of thirty, He knew it was time for Him to begin the work for which He had been born: to tell the world about the love of God and show them the way to become His children.

Because Jesus was God as well as a man, He could do wonderful, miraculous things—things that seemed impossible. When He touched blind people, they could see. When He told sickness to leave, it disappeared. Jesus' words held power over every created thing. Whatever He spoke came to be.

The most important thing that Jesus said was that He was God's Son—the long-awaited Messiah that the prophets had foretold. Jesus' claim made many people extremely angry, especially the ones who considered themselves wise and important. They couldn't imagine that this poor carpenter could possibly be the Messiah.

The Messiah they expected was a powerful, impressive person who would take over the world, not this average, ordinary man. They thought that Jesus was either a common liar, or that He was completely insane. But Jesus said many times that God was His Father, and He made it clear that He was the fulfillment of the ancient prophecies.

Just as in Jesus' time, there are people today who don't believe that Jesus is God's Son. There is no denying that Jesus truly impacted the world. The things He taught have become the standard for acceptable behavior. Even the numbering of years is based upon His birth.

Some people believe Jesus was a prophet. Some think He was a genius with knowledge and wisdom beyond others of His time. But the fact of the matter is that if Jesus was not the Son of God, then He was a liar. And if He didn't realize He was lying, then He was totally insane.[1]

Since nearly everyone over the centuries has agreed that Jesus was filled with wisdom and great understanding, how could He be a sinful liar? Even though Jesus walked the earth over 2,000 years ago, He is still admired and His teachings are accepted as absolute truth. How could He still be admired if He were only a crazy lunatic?

The only other choice is that He is exactly who He claimed to be: the Messiah, the Son of Almighty God!

So let's take a closer look at this amazing Man. What did He do while He was alive on earth that made "Jesus" a name that EVERYONE knows? What does it mean that He died for you? How can you really know Him and talk with Him?

WHO IS THIS JESUS?

1. The Liar, Lunatic, or Lord reasoning is credited to C.S. Lewis as found in his book *Mere Christianity* (© 1943 C. Lewis); and Josh McDowell as found in his book *More Than a Carpenter* (© 1977, 2005 Josh McDowell)

Jesus Is...

To prepare for this session, listen to the **WORD OF PROMISE** New Testament recording of:

Book of Matthew, chapters 1 & 2

Book of Luke, chapters 1 & 2

Throughout the Bible, Jesus is called by many names. Each one tells us a bit more about who He is and the unique purpose assigned to Him by God—His ministry.

In this "Hear It" section of Scripture, Jesus is given at least nine different names. Let's take a look at them and discover what they mean.

JESUS – This name was an ancient one which means "He Shall Save."

CHRIST – The name "Christ" is actually a title. Calling Jesus "the Christ" is much like saying, "President Obama." When you hear the word "president" you automatically know what that means. The word "Christ" means the One who is the "Messiah." So when you say "Jesus Christ," you are actually telling the world that Jesus is the Messiah, the Son of God.

IMMANUEL – This name literally means "God with us."

KING OF THE JEWS –The world began to realize who Jesus was as soon as He was born. Even the stars proclaimed that a King had been given to the world. Jesus is King of all creation, for all time. But His kingdom is a spiritual one, not an earthly one. We'll learn more about this later.

RULER – Because Jesus is God's Son, He has authority over everything that exists. He is the ultimate Ruler.

SON OF THE MOST HIGH – In the Old Testament, God is often called "Most High God" or "God Most High." This means that God is above all things, not just physically, but in all ways. He is greater than anything else that exists. Because Jesus is the Son of God, He is also greater than every other thing.

LORD – Lord is a word that is not used often in today's world. But people long ago understood it well. In times past, a Lord was one who owned everything. His power was absolute and His word was law.

SAVIOR – This word refers to someone who rescues another. A savior is a deliverer; one who preserves the life of another. Jesus is the Savior of the world. He rescues us from the penalty of sin and delivers us from death.

SALVATION – The meanings of this word are many and powerful. It means happiness, well-being, deliverance, and rescue. Because this name is given to Jesus, we know He will provide all this for us.

CHRIST

Thus there were fourteen generations in all from Abraham to David, fourteen from David to the exile to Babylon, and fourteen from the exile to the Christ.

Matthew 1:17

The list below contains only a few of the names that Jesus has been given. As we listen to more of the New Testament, we will discover many more. Within this game there are 20 names of Jesus. *Locate and circle as many as you can find.*

```
D  G  O  L  O  R  E  T  S  A  M  T  H  E  E  V
E  S  Z  B  M  A  R  T  E  A  C  H  E  R  Q  R
L  O  S  N  A  M  J  K  C  R  H  E  I  E  B  O
I  N  P  U  L  T  E  H  M  X  R  T  Z  D  R  L
V  O  W  V  F  M  X  S  K  H  I  R  S  E  O  E
E  F  N  L  C  P  J  E  S  U  S  U  O  E  I  S
R  G  D  O  R  D  M  Z  W  I  T  T  R  M  V  N
E  O  O  L  T  H  E  W  A  Y  A  H  W  E  A  U
R  D  R  O  L  O  R  M  Y  X  P  H  Z  R  S  O
E  X  U  I  Q  B  H  O  L  Y  O  N  E  V  A  C
V  W  P  R  I  N  C  E  O  F  P  E  A  C  E  I
I  O  A  S  W  E  J  E  H  T  F  O  G  N  I  K
L  F  G  P  I  M  M  A  N  U  E  L  D  G  O  L
E  A  S  H  E  P  H  E  R  D  L  M  B  Q  R  S
D  Z  S  O  N  O  F  M  A  N  P  W  Z  R  L  N
U  X  V  R  T  O  L  L  U  F  R  E  D  N  O  W
```

Jesus	Messiah	The Truth	Savior
Son of God	The Way	Counselor	Son of Man
Lord	Master	Prince of Peace	Deliverer
Teacher	Shepherd	Wonderful	Holy One
Christ	King of the Jews	Redeemer	Immanuel

Check your answers in the Answer Key at the end of this book

GRAB IT!

Have you ever looked at a book of names and their meanings? Most names have a "definition" just like any other word. Here are a few examples:

JOHN means "Yahweh (God) is gracious."

CHRISTINA means "Christian."

ADAM means "man."

NICOLE means "victory."

TIMOTHY means "honoring God."

EMMA means "universal."

In ancient times, the meaning of names was considered very important. Parents were careful to give names to their children that spoke of their desire for the child's future, or sometimes, contained the insight God had given of that child's character or unique purpose in life. At times, God actually changed the names of certain people whose lives would be used in a special way.

All the names of Jesus tell us something about Him. Each one gives us an insight into what He can and should be in our lives.

- Because He is called "**JESUS**," we know He can save us from all the darkness and evil in the world.
- Because He is called "**THE CHRIST**," we can be certain that He is the One sent by God to bring us into a special relationship with God.
- Because He is called "**IMMANUEL**," there is no doubt that God desires a close, personal relationship with us.
- Because He is called "**KING OF THE JEWS**," we know He has a kingdom prepared for His people.
- Because He is called "**RULER**," it is certain that Jesus is the absolute authority in all things.
- Because He is called "**SON OF THE MOST HIGH**," we know Jesus is greater than and high above all created things.
- Because He is called "**LORD**," we can be sure that nothing on earth is more powerful than Jesus.
- Because He is called "**SAVIOR**," we know that Jesus has provided the way for us to be free from the effects of sin.
- Because He is called "**SALVATION**," there is nothing that should be able to defeat us. Jesus is the rescuer!

HOLD IT!

So now we have an idea of who Jesus is and why God sent Him to earth. But if all this is only information to be learned and stored up in your mind, it really won't make any difference at all in your life. If you learn how to do math problems but never use math in your daily life, what use is the knowledge? If you one day learn to drive, but never get behind the wheel of a car, then knowing how to drive really has no meaning.

It is the same with learning about Jesus. If you only learn the facts about Him, you don't really know Jesus. The facts are just stored-up knowledge with no power to change your life. But Jesus came to earth so that you could live a life that is filled with all the wonderful gifts He came to give.

The next time you find yourself tempted to do something wrong, remember that Jesus is "God with Us." He can help you say "NO" to those things that are wrong. If you begin to feel that the world is an ugly place and filled with sadness, just think about Jesus, your Salvation. He will bring peace and joy, even when the world looks depressing or hopeless. When you feel lonely, He is Immanuel. When you feel weak and helpless and the world seems to be against you, He is your Lord. When you wish you had a different life, He is King of the Jews. He is Ruler when you need an answer. And when you're lost and not sure what to do or what is right, He is Savior.

Whatever you need, Jesus holds the answer. He is the Messiah—the God-man promised in the past, with you today, and the one who holds the future in His hands.

LIVE IT!

CAN YOU IMAGINE how wonderful it would be to be able to actually have a conversation with the One who created you? He knows everything about you, so He could answer all your questions. There is nothing more powerful than Him, so He could always help you defeat the problems in your life.

If that sounds like a great thing to you, I have good news! Because Jesus came to earth, you can know God!

Here's how it works:

Adam and Eve were the first people God created. They were perfect in every way: physically, mentally, and spiritually. There was no disease and no death. Their relationship with God was so close that God actually visited them daily. They had the opportunity to talk with Him and spend time getting to know the One who had created them. They knew beyond a doubt that God loved them.

God wanted to know that Adam and Eve loved Him, so He gave them one rule: they could eat anything that grew in the garden except the fruit of one tree. God realized that if Adam and Eve loved Him only because they had no choice, then it wasn't really love. So He gave them the option of choosing to love and obey Him.

But Adam and Eve chose to disobey God's one and only rule. They ate the fruit of the forbidden tree. This act told God that they did not really love Him. The relationship between them was broken and sin (the wrong attitude that causes people to disobey God) was born. Because of sin, sickness, pain, and death entered the world. But not just physical death; sin caused Adam and Eve to die spiritually. That incredible glow of knowing God so intimately became dark. And that inner part of them that had been connected completely to God, died.

From that time on, all people have had hearts that are ruled by sin. All of us are incapable of living our lives in the right way—completely connected to God. And because God is absolutely holy, He cannot even look at sinful things. So people became totally separated from God, spiritually dead without a way to be made alive again.

God was heartbroken that His people had been disconnected from Him. He spoke to them through prophets and sent many signs to them to let them know His love for them had not ended.

Then God sent Jesus to be born into the world. Jesus was completely God, so He was completely holy. He was completely man, so He was the first completely holy man since before Adam sinned. His relationship with God was close and personal, just like Adam's had been. Because He was holy, He was not under the curse of death like other men. Because He was God, He loved all people and wanted to provide them with a way to reconnected to God.

So Jesus voluntarily took upon Himself the curse of death: spiritual and physical. He allowed Himself to be killed so that He could die in your place. He rose from death so that He could give you a life completely connected to God. You only need to believe and accept that what Jesus did, He did for you. It's called being born again. Because sin has brought spiritual death, and Jesus brings spiritual life, it is like being born into a brand new world. And this new world is the kingdom of Almighty God.

If you would like to begin this entirely new life in God's kingdom and be able to really know God, then read the following prayer. If you truly mean it with your heart, then when it is finished, you will become a brand new person and a whole new world will open up to you.

Pray[er]

FATHER GOD,

I want to know you. I want to be born into your kingdom. I believe in your Son and all that He has done for me. I know His death has bought my freedom from the penalty of sin and death. I know I am now free to come to you and ask for new life in Jesus. Forgive me, Father, for all the sin in my heart. Please remove it from me and help me to live as Jesus taught us to live. Please accept me as your child and let me be born into the eternal kingdom of God. I thank you and praise you for all you are and for all you've done. I ask you all this in the name of Jesus the Christ.

Amen

NAME GAME

CONNECT THE NAME

Let's see if you've understood all that Jesus can mean to you. In the first column below, you will find the names of Jesus. In the second column, "For Me," you will find a way that Jesus can help you through life. *Match the letter of the "For Me" answer with the appropriate "Name of Jesus."*

	Name of Jesus		For Me...
	The Christ	A	Jesus will always give me the answer, even when things seem impossible.
	Immanuel	B	Jesus is there when I need someone to care that I am sad and lonely.
	Savior	C	Jesus will forgive me when I have done something wrong.
	Salvation	D	Jesus helps me be content in my world.
	Ruler	E	Jesus will help me know God.
	King of the Jews	F	Jesus will always be there when I need Him.
	Lord	G	Jesus knows what it is like to be a human, so He can help me know what is right.
	Son of the Most High	H	Jesus will help me when it seems like the world is against me.

Check your answers in the Answer Key at the end of this book

welcome to the Kingdom of God!!!!!

[Now write the date and time you prayed this prayer. It's almost like a birth certificate. This little record will remind you of the exact moment you became a citizen of God's kingdom.]

RECORD OF NEW BIRTH

_____   _____
Date   Time

_____   _____
First Name   Last Name

_____
Location

GIVE IT

NOW THAT YOU ARE A CITIZEN of God's kingdom, it's time to share the good news! It's like you have found a treasure that is more valuable than all the gold on earth. You just have to let other people know!

Tell a family member or a friend about this incredible thing that has happened to you. Tell them about Jesus and all He can do for them. What a wonderful gift to give someone you care about.

Jesus is: the Christ, Son of the Most High, Savior, Salvation, Immanuel, King of the Jews, Ruler and Lord!

MESSAGE FROM THE *WORD OF PROMISE*

Locate the letter in the following grid which corresponds with the number below. You will discover a powerful message from Jesus. *Try to memorize it. His words hold power to change your heart and life.*

A	B	C	D	E	F	G	H	I	J	K	L	M
1	2	3	4	5	6	7	8	9	10	11	12	13

N	O	P	Q	R	S	T	U	V	W	X	Y	Z
14	15	16	17	18	19		21	22	23		25	

"...— — — — — — — — — — — — — — — — — — — —
   9 3 1 13 5   20 15   7 9 22 5   12 9 6 5   12 9 6 5   9 14

— — —   — — '— — — — — — — — —."
 1 12 12   9 20 19   6 21 12 12 14 5 19 19   (John 10:10)

Check your answers in the Answer Key at the end of this book

To prepare for this session, listen to the *WORD OF PROMISE* New Testament recording of:

Book of Matthew, chapters 3 & 4

Book of Mark, chapter 1

Book of Luke, chapters 3 & 4

When some new show, concert, or movie is created, news about it travels fast. We find it advertised everywhere: on television, on radio, and announcements can be found all over the Internet.

The "Get It" chapters for this session tell about the "advertising" God arranged to let the world know that Jesus had come. Obviously, there were no newspapers, and certainly no television or Internet during those days; so God sent a man named John to spread the news. And just like an advertisement is designed to catch your attention, God designed John to be hard to miss.

John grew up knowing that God had a very special purpose for him. That knowledge would have set him apart from other children and most likely caused John to be a much more serious child. He knew he had a job to do and spent his early life preparing to do exactly what God requested—announce the coming of the Messiah—Jesus, the Savior of the world.

Whatever the cause, the adult John was quite different from other people; actually he was a bit weird. He lived alone in the wild, mountainous area near where he had been born. The only food he ate was whatever he could find and kill. He wore clothes which he most likely made himself from the skins of camels. Having no real home, John did not possess anything to keep himself groomed. Try to picture how he must have looked!

John looked strange, acted strangely, and even ate strange food. In some ways, it may seem odd that God chose him to "advertise" that Jesus had come to save the world. But it's easy to see why John got everyone's attention!

God sent a man named John to spread the news about Jesus.

FIND THE PROPHECY

Long before John was born, his life and ministry were predicted by a prophet. Complete the game below to learn where to locate this prophecy in the Bible.

Start with the blue letter near the center of the grid below and then follow the directions. As you locate the correct letters or numbers, write them in the space provided below.

30	A	2	R	A	S	1	25	B	W
L	33	M	X	T	K	A	7	U	P
B	O	I	C	V	52	E	3	R	9
A	21	M	S	P	R	L	74	C	D
J	K	16	M	H	I	S	10	A	P
4	O	40	B	U	W	X	K	B	N
O	5	M	S	X	Q	Z	41	F	I
R	O	C	33	I	8	40	S	9	A
92	P	Z	M	3	W	R	E	B	5
A	I	7	H	85	V	L	K	67	M

Answer: __ __ __ __ __ __ __:__, __, __

Start with the blue letter.   I

Go down two spaces and left 2 spaces. _____

Go up 6 spaces and right 1 space. _____

Go down 2 spaces and left 2 spaces. _____

Go down 2 spaces and right 6 spaces. _____

Go down 5 spaces and left 5 spaces. _____

Go up 4 spaces and left 1 space. _____

Go up 3 spaces and right 5 spaces. _____

Go down 3 spaces and left 7 spaces. _____

Go down 3 spaces and right 9 spaces. _____

Read this part of the Old Testament. Check your answers in the Answer Key at the end of this book

GRAB IT!

John had a job to do and he gave it all the energy he had to give. God had told him the truth about Jesus and John wanted the world to know. Many messages had been sent by God to prophets throughout the centuries, but John's message was the most important and most life-changing. He was given the honor of announcing to the world that Jesus was the Messiah.

Can you even imagine what it would be like to actually hear God speak to you as John did? Well, there's good news for you! He still speaks to people today! The best way you can hear God's voice is through His Word, the Bible. The Bible is a book that comes straight from God. Although people actually wrote down the words, God told them what to say. In the pages of the Bible you can find answers to your questions and the perfect guide to living a meaningful, successful life.

God can also speak to you in other ways. He can speak wisdom to you through parents, teachers, family, and friends. He gave you a conscience, that part deep inside of you that warns you when you are doing wrong. He created a world that will speak to you of His love and incredible power. And, if you listen closely, you may hear a quiet voice inside your heart that will lead you to make right choices and help you learn about God's plan for your life.

HOLD IT!

The Bible is a huge book that can really seem tough to read and even harder to understand. But God put in it all the answers and direction you will ever need throughout your entire life.

By reading the Bible, you will learn why things in the world can be difficult and how to make the right decisions. You will discover stories about people who lived long ago, but had some of the same struggles and problems you face today. Their stories can help you find a way to handle your own difficult times.

But the most amazing reason to read the Bible is that it will tell you about God's plan for your life. You can be like John and know exactly why God created you and what He wants in your future. No matter which occupation you choose, God has a bigger plan in mind for you. He wants you to live as a child of His kingdom and tell the world the Messiah has come.

DISCOVER THE NEW TESTAMENT

The list below includes the names of all 27 books of the New Testament (the part of the Bible that begins with Jesus). See if you can complete the list by adding the missing vowels (a, e, i, o, u). *Try to complete the names without looking at a Bible.*

MTTHW   _____

MRK   _____

LK   _____

JHN   _____

CTS   _____

RMNS   _____

1 CRNTHNS   _____

2 CRNTHNS   _____

GLTNS   _____

PHSNS   _____

PHLPPNS   _____

CLSSNS   _____

1 THSSLNNS   _____

2 THSSLNNS   _____

1 TMTHY   _____

2 TMTHY   _____

TTS   _____

PHLMN   _____

HBRWS   _____

JMS   _____

1 PTR   _____

2 PTR   _____

1 JHN   _____

2 JHN   _____

3 JHN   _____

JD   _____

RVLTN   _____

Check your answers in the Answer Key at the end of this book

THE BEST WAY to get an answer to any question is to ask someone who knows the answer. And when it comes to making the right choices and discovering God's unique plan for you, the only who knows the whole answer is God.

Just like God told John's father exactly who his son would become, God has given your parents a special insight into who you are and the best choices for you to make. It can seem unfair sometimes that our parents always have the final word. But God has entrusted them with the responsibility of making sure we learn everything we need to know to be adults ourselves. As hard as it might be at times, it's always best to listen to them. They've had a longer time to learn to hear from God and they know how difficult life can be when we make wrong choices.

Think of it this way; if you are going on a trip, you use a map. Someone traveled to the same place and made a record of the roads. If you follow their directions, you will get exactly where you want to go. But if you decide you want to do it your own way, you may never get there. And if you should eventually arrive, it will have taken much longer, because you didn't know where the roads would lead. God has taken your parents along the same roads, and they have learned the right way. Why get lost, when you can follow the map?

de·fine [*it*]

BIBLE: A collection of 66 books written by different men throughout history, but all divinely inspired by God (God controlled what they wrote and actually wrote it through them). Christians believe that everything in the Bible is true and will never change—that the Bible is "living and active." This means that its truth still applies to us today, and that God uses it to speak to us. The Bible is the Word of God; you can trust it and believe every word. (Taken/edited from Revolve volume 1)

de·fine [*it*]

OBEDIENCE: This word is used in the Bible quite often. The biblical meaning is to listen closely with respect, to be agreeable and willing to follow instruction. Obedience is an important part of being a Christian. It is extremely important to obey God and the people God has placed in our lives to lead us the right way.

WORD GAME

IN OBEDIENCE

See how many words you can find that are contained in the word "obedience." You may use each letter only once in each word. *Each word must have at least 3 letters.*

OBEDIENCE

_____   _____
_____   _____
_____   _____
_____   _____
_____   _____
_____   _____
_____   _____
_____   _____
_____   _____
_____   _____

GIVE IT

EVERY DAY THINGS HAPPEN that force you to make choices. Are you going to listen in class or cause trouble? Will you do your homework or play games instead? Are you going to do what you know your parents would want or are you going to let others convince you to choose another way?

The entire New Testament part of the Bible tells us about Jesus. His words will tell you all about how to live as God wants you to and to make choices that please Him. If you will listen to Him you will be able to avoid problems and bad situations that happen because of bad decisions. A good question to ask yourself (or others) when you have a choice to make is: "What would Jesus do?"

Why not spend one entire day trying to do only those things you know God wants you to do? See what a difference it can make in your life to follow God's "map" for your life.

MESSAGE FROM THE *WORD OF PROMISE*

Locate the letter in the following grid which corresponds with the symbol below. You will discover a powerful message from the Bible. *Try to memorize it.* The Word of God is our guide to living our lives in the way God wants.

A	B	C	D	E	F	G	H	I	J	K	L	M
▲	#	↕	&	•	■	*	~	◊	<	>	^	«

N	O	P	Q	R	S	T	U	V	W	X	Y	Z
◄	{	[	}	]	ψ	/	—	▼	►	₪	▫	↔

Jesus said: "__ __ __ __ __ __ __ __ __ __ __ __
    « ▫   « { / ~ •]   ▲ ◄ & « ▫

__ __ __ __ __ __ __ __ __ __ __ __ __ __ __ __
] { / ~ •] ψ ▲] • / ~ { ψ •

__ __ __ __ __ __ __ __ __ __ __ __ __ __ __ __ ,
► ~ { ^ ◊ ψ / • ◄ / { * { & ψ

__ __ __ __ __ __ __ __ __ __ __ __ __ __ __ __!"
/ • ▲ ↕ ~ ◊ ◄ * ▲ ◄ & { # • ▫ ◊ /

(Luke 8:21)

Check your answers in the Answer Key at the end of this book

God's Plan

To prepare for this session, listen to the **WORD OF PROMISE** New Testament recording of:

hear it!

Book of Matthew, chapters 5 & 6

Book of Mark, chapters 2 and 3

Book of Luke, chapters 5 & 6

Attitude. You read about it and hear about it from adults all the time. You may get scolded for a bad one or praised for a good one. You can have one, give one, receive one, and even "cop" one. But what on earth is an attitude? And what makes it such a big deal?

An attitude is the way you react *inside* yourself to things *outside*. It's the feeling or way of thinking that results in the way you behave. Others can tell you about it, and request you change it; but your attitude is something only you can control.

You just listened to the parts of Scripture that contain one of the first sermons Jesus ever taught. Obviously, He considered this an important message. It is often referred to as the "Beatitudes." Another way of thinking of this sermon is the "BE attitudes." They are Jesus' directions to us on the right ways of thinking and responding to people and situations—the way you should "Be."

Jesus said many times that the people who have a right attitude will be "happy." But this kind of happiness is not the same as the way you feel when you are acting silly or after you get a great new gift. It's a kind of happiness that doesn't go away. It's a lasting feeling that has nothing to do with what goes on outside of you. This happiness comes from the inside, no matter what's happening on the outside.

The biggest difference about this kind of happiness is that it comes from your own decision. Whenever anything happens to you, you have a choice about how you will react. And your reactions will come directly from the way you allow yourself to think. If you think angry thoughts, you will act angry and your whole attitude will become unfriendly and cold. But if you refuse to allow yourself to think those angry thoughts and choose to find good, positive things to think about, your attitude will also be positive. You will have chosen to be "happy."

Your attitude is what determines the way you respond to other people. It also determines how you will respond to God. Of all the things in life, God and others are the most important. You can be sure that's one of the reasons Jesus chose this as one of the first things He taught to the world.

WHAT'S THE ATTITUDE?

Below you will find two columns of words that have been scrambled. The first column contains negative attitudes, and the second contains positive attitudes. See if you can unscramble them. *In the spaces provided at the end, see how many more positive and negative attitudes you can add.*

NEGATIVE	ANSWER	POSITIVE	ANSWER
UEBELRIOSL	_____	TODEBINE	_____
GRANY	_____	BULHEM	_____
RUCANNIG	_____	GLIVON	_____
DROPU	_____	RIDEFLYN	_____
LISHSEF	_____	LUPFLEH	_____
	_____		_____
	_____		_____
	_____		_____
	_____		_____
	_____		_____

Check your answers in the Answer Key at the end of this book

GRAB IT!

Take a look at the negative attitude list above. What do they have in common? Someone with a bad attitude always thinks of themselves first. They are always #1, no one else is important.

Someone who has a rebellious attitude wants to do what they want, when they want, no matter what anyone else thinks.

Someone who has an angry attitude thinks they have been wronged—their feelings and their wants are most important.

Someone with an uncaring attitude thinks only of themselves and never someone else.

Get the idea?

It's difficult to deal with people with a bad attitude. Someone who thinks only of themselves can make life difficult for everyone around them. They let their feelings tell them what to do instead of considering what is right. Jesus made it clear that our attitudes are important, but those with a negative attitude don't seem to get it. They are too busy thinking of themselves.

Now look at the positive attitude list. The one thing they have in common is they all focus on someone else's wants and needs.

If you have an obedient attitude, you want to please those who are in authority.

If you have a humble attitude, you always put others first.

If your attitude is loving, you try to do what is best for others.

It's not easy to always think of others first. You have to really pay attention to the things you say and do and how it affects those around you. And you have to be determined to act with a positive attitude. You have to take the time to make the right decision and not let your feelings rule your actions.

Jesus is the perfect example of how to live with a positive attitude. Everything He did and everything He said was for the good of other people. He taught them, He healed them, He loved them, and He died for them. A right attitude always puts others first.

HOLD IT! None of us could live our lives without other people. Think about it: if there were no other people in the world, you wouldn't be able to learn how to be a friend, or a student, or an adult. There would be no one to talk to and no one to learn from. You would never learn how to love or how to laugh. All the best things in life, besides God, could never be. And you couldn't even have the same kind of relationship with Him, because there would be no one for you to share the joy of knowing Him.

It's plain to see that you need other people in your life. In the good times they share your joy and in the bad times they help you through. In a very real way, other people make life worth living. Imagine what it would be like to have no one in your life to tell about the good things that happen to you. Or how lonely it would be to have no one to care when you're hurting. Your attitude will determine what your life becomes. It can draw people to you or drive them away.

It isn't always easy to keep a positive attitude. We talked earlier about learning to listen to God's voice and follow the words of Jesus so that we can make right choices. Even when we listen closely and try to do what Jesus would do, it can be difficult to learn exactly what those right choices are. But, it can be even more difficult to actually learn to make the right choice—to act on what you know is right. So when it comes to keeping a right attitude, it is very important to listen for the voice of God—through the words of Jesus, through other people, or from deep inside your heart.

No one can keep negative things from happening, or always keep themselves from making bad choices. But God will always be there to help you and guide you, no matter what happens. Just listen closely, He'll tell you the right way.

WORD GAME

FIND THE PROMISE

"T_ _ _e w_ _ w_ _t t_ _o

r_ _ _t _ _ re th _ _ anyt_ _ _g

el_ _ _ _e h_ _ _y. G_ _ _ _ll

_ _ _ ly sa_ _ _fy th_ _." (Matthew 5:6)

The words in this Bible quote have missing letter groups. All the letters needed to finish the words can be found in the list below. *See if you can complete the words to find a promise from Jesus to you.*

ful	igh	d	mo	od	se
an	em	wi	tis	hos	app
o	hin	ar	ho	an	

Check your answers in the Answer Key at the end of this book

LIVE IT!

THERE'S NO DOUBT that it can be really hard to always have a right attitude. It takes a lot of work and time to learn to make our thoughts go into right places. But even when we begin to learn how to keep our own attitude positive, someone else's bad attitude can really put us to the test. When someone has made us unhappy or caused us problems, it can make us want to treat them the same. No one likes to be hurt or suffer wrongly because of someone else. And it's awful to have someone spread their bad attitude around. If they're going to be difficult, they don't deserve to be treated well, right?

At the very end of the "Hear It" Bible listening for this session, you heard Jesus' words, "Do for others what you want them to do for you." This is called the "Golden Rule." It is one of the most important guides Jesus gave us for keeping a positive attitude toward others. Just because someone treats you badly, it doesn't give you the right to treat them the same way. Think about it. If everyone always chose to treat others in the way they wanted to be treated, what kind of world would it be?

It may seem that just one person making the choice to live with a positive attitude and treat others well won't really make much of a difference in the world. But changes happen slowly—one choice at a time. Look at Martin Luther King, or Mother Teresa, or Billy Graham. They are examples of one person with a positive attitude making the world a better place for all of us. Each one of them learned how to keep their attitude toward others right and treated all people in the way they wanted others to treat them; even if others were cruel or unkind.

One of the people reading this may be the Abraham Lincoln of tomorrow. Maybe you will become the next Billy Graham or Mother Teresa. The only one who can stop you from becoming a person who can make the world a better place is you.

GIVE IT

JESUS SPENT HIS LIFE giving to other people and taught us what it means to put other people first. He showed us how the "Golden Rule" can change lives and even change the world—one life at a time.

Now that you understand how important a positive attitude is, go back and listen to Matthew 5. See if you can find the positive attitudes in Jesus' words. Then make a decision that, just for today, you will try to make choices based on what you heard.

In what ways can you have a positive attitude and live out the "Golden Rule" with the people listed below?

- Your parents
- Your best friend
- Someone who hurt you
- Your brother or sister
- A stranger

Now go do the things you thought of. You could start a chain reaction; your positive attitude could spread to everyone around you. Try it and see if your world doesn't become just a little better. Then try it again tomorrow. What have you got to lose?

WORD GAME

MESSAGE FROM *THE WORD OF PROMISE*

Fill in the right letter in the blanks below to discover the message from Jesus. See if you can figure out the missing letters.

For New Life

T	R	I	S	U	C	E	G	A	L	W
1	2	3	4	5	6	7	8	9	10	11

O	V	F	N	P	D	G	Y	H	B
12	13	14	15	16	17	18	19	20	21

"...___ ___ ___   ___   ___ ___ ___ ___   ___   ___ ___   ___ ___
  19 12 5   4   12 5 10 17   7   10 3   20 1

___ ___ ___ ___   ___ ___   ___ ___ ___ ___ . ___ ___   ___
14   2   12 1   7 2   7 12 16 10   10 3   7

___ ___ ___ ___   ___ ___ ___   ___ ___ ___ ___ ___
4 12 1 20   1 20 7   3 10 10 4 7

___ ___ ___   ___ ___ ___ ___   ___ ___ ___ ___ ___ .
1 7 8   17 1 20 3   4 19 12 5 17

(Matthew 5:16)

Check your answers in the Answer Key at the end of this book

To prepare for this session, listen to the **WORD OF PROMISE** New Testament recording of:

hear it!

Book of Matthew, chapters 7 & 8

Book of Mark, chapters 4 & 5

Book of Luke, chapters 7 & 8

You learned earlier that Jesus gave His life so that you could be reconnected to God and have a new, eternal life as a child of God. The key to receiving the new life God has for you is forgiveness. You must come to God and admit that sin is in your heart—even when you try to live in the right way, you do wrong things and make wrong choices that hurt others and displease God. But just admitting that you are sinful is not enough. You have to want to change.

de·fine [it]

ETERNAL: Something eternal has no beginning and no end. It is something that never changes and will exist forever.

It's like this:

Imagine you are walking down a path and right in front of you a deep pit filled with quicksand appears. In order to keep walking on the path you have to somehow get over the quicksand. It looks harmless and you think you can walk on top of it, so you continue walking. But with every step you sink deeper into the quicksand. Soon you are stuck and helpless to get yourself out. Now imagine someone comes along and pulls you out of the slimy quicksand. You are so thrilled to be rescued! Then the one who saved you helps you get cleaned up and gives you new clothes to put on. You're clean and refreshed and ready to start walking again. Instead of turning around and finding another path, you decide to try walking over the quicksand again. Guess what happens. That's right; you're soon sinking into the pit again.

Sin is just like that quicksand pit in your path. Even after you have been born again and forgiven for the sin in your heart, you can still choose to act in ways that don't please God. As you make choices you may discover that the path you're traveling leads straight into the dirty, dangerous pit of sin. It might look harmless and you may think it can't really hurt you. So you may choose to keep walking into the sin. If you do, just as if it were quicksand, you will find yourself completely stuck in the filthy mess. The sin would act just like quicksand and you would soon find yourself totally stuck and helpless to get yourself out. When you ask, Jesus will always rescue you, clean you up, and make things right again. But if you don't turn around and go in another direction, as soon as you start walking, you will fall right back in. You have to decide to go another way.

That's the way sin operates. No matter how sorry you are that you fell in it, if you don't turn around and choose another way, you will end up stuck again.

de·fine [it]

REPENT: This word means to change your mind and your direction. It means to regret your behavior and make a decision to turn around and go in a better way.

The way to avoid getting caught in sin over and over is to ask to be forgiven (like being saved from the quicksand and getting cleaned up) and then repent (turn around and go another way). When you ask to be forgiven without really meaning to change, it's like you have already decided to walk into the quicksand again.

START HERE

FINISH

Check your answers in the Answer Key at the end of this book

Free from Sin's Power

GRAB IT!

God gave us the Bible to tell us how to live a life that pleases Him. Since He is the One who created us, He is the only One who really knows how life was meant to be lived. His rules are meant to help us live successful lives free from sin, not to make our lives harder or keep us from having fun. God's rules keep us from hurting ourselves or others and teach us the difference between right and wrong.

If you could follow your family's generations all the way back in time, far past great-grandparents and great-great-grandparents, you would find that Adam and Eve are in your family tree. They were the first parents and all people, living and dead, came from them. When Adam and Eve disobeyed God their hearts became dark and dirty with sin; so all the people born after them are born with the same sin-filled heart. Jesus died so that we could be born again and receive a new, clean heart. This new heart doesn't have to be ruled by sin like our old one, it is meant to be ruled by God.

Even after we are born again and have this new heart, we can still choose to disobey God's rules. Every time we have a decision to make about our behavior or our attitude, we can choose God's way or another way. If we don't choose God's way, we have sinned.

God gave us the Bible, His Word, so we could know His rules and how to live without sin. He sent Jesus, not only to bring us new life, but to teach us how to live it in the right way. It's important to know what the Bible says and the things Jesus taught so we can know the right way to live.

Even when we choose the wrong way and disobey God, He will always forgive us because Jesus gave His life to pay for our sin. Even if we really mess up and make a horrible choice, because of Jesus, God will still forgive us as soon as we ask and repent. Nothing we can do is too big for Him to forgive.

GRAB IT! NOTE

Now you understand what it means be born again. You also know that once you begin this new life you can still make wrong choices. Even then, you only need to repent and receive forgiveness from God. But your attitude can really make a difference when it comes to forgiveness.

The wrong attitude will cause you to tell God you're sorry and ask for forgiveness without ever meaning to turn your behavior around and repent. That usually means you're sorry you got caught, not that you're sorry for doing the wrong thing. That's really a selfish attitude—you're just doing whatever makes everything work out best for you.

When you ask God to forgive you because you really know what you did was wrong, and you choose to act in another way, then you're operating with the right attitude—the attitude that cares more about what God wants than what you want.

HOLD IT!

To understand how to make right choices, it's important for you to understand who Satan is. God loved him and created him to be extremely intelligent and talented. He was an angel in heaven (God's home) with great power and intelligence, more than any other angel. Soon Satan began to think he was as great as God and should have his own kingdom. His attitude got worse and worse until he didn't care what God thought or whether he broke God's rules. He didn't care that God loved him or what the consequences of disobedience might be. He decided to do whatever he wished, no matter what. Satan was the first being who rebelled against God.

Because Satan rebelled against God and chose to think only about himself, God forced him to leave heaven. Satan was extremely angry with God and wanted to hurt Him. His opportunity came when God created Adam and Eve. Because God loved them, Satan hated them and decided to hurt God by hurting them. Satan convinced Adam and Eve to disobey God, and the whole mess of sin began.

We've heard in earlier "Hear It" sections how Satan tried to convince Jesus to sin. (This is called being "tempted.") But Jesus always chose to do what was right in God's eyes. By refusing to listen to Satan, Jesus was able to live totally without sin. He knew that God's love will never end.

Jesus is perfect, but people are not—not you, not your parents, not your teachers; no one! No one can live everyday without ever making wrong choices. That's because Satan hates whatever God loves, so he tries to get people to hurt themselves and others by sinning. It's not like in the movies where a horrible demonic character shows up and speaks in an animal-like voice. We would all realize that was evil and wrong. Satan likes to stay hidden; so he just tries to make us think wrong thoughts, or he whispers ideas to us that can lead us to do wrong things.

Whenever you are tempted to make a wrong decision, think about what you've read here. Always take the time to ask yourself if the choice you're about to make will hurt someone else or cause you to disobey God's rules. Then think about how Jesus would handle the situation and ask Him to help you do what's right.

IT'S IN THERE

The idea of "forgiveness" is one that holds many truths. There are also many other words that you can make using the same letters. Below you will find nine sentences with missing words. Each of the missing words can be found using the letters of "forgiveness." See if you can fill in the missing word. *When you have located all ten, see how many more words you can find. Remember, each letter can be used only one time.*

FORGIVENESS

Because of __ __ __ in my heart, I need God's forgiveness.

Jesus gave His life __ __ __ me.

Believing in Jesus __ __ __ __ __ me eternal life.

When I admit my sin and repent, God __ __ __ __ __ __ __ __ me.

Jesus has __ __ __ __ __ me the promise of new life in Him.

Everyone has sinned and needs to be __ __ __ __ __ __ __ __

God will __ __ __ __ __ refuse to forgive me when I ask and repent.

God will not __ __ __ __ stop loving me.

Jesus will forgive me __ __ __ __ when I really mess up.

Because I have been forgiven, I should __ __ __ __ forgiveness to others.

_____

_____

_____

_____

_____

_____

_____

_____

_____

_____

Check your answers in the Answer Key at the end of this book

ISN'T IT GREAT that you can be forgiven by simply asking God and choosing another way to behave?

The best part about God's forgiveness is that it's absolutely complete. God's love is so huge that He never holds our bad choices against us if we ask to be forgiven and we repent. But He doesn't just forgive, He totally forgets that we ever sinned! It's like it never happened!

You've heard that Jesus says you should forgive others in exactly the same way that God forgives. When another person does something that hurts you and asks you to forgive them, you have a choice to make. You can truly forgive, or you can refuse. Even if you say the words "you're forgiven" it doesn't mean a lot if you remain angry inside or if you constantly remember what hurt you. While it's true that you can't totally forget like God can, you can choose to force your thoughts toward good, positive things. You can remember all the laughs and good times you've had with the one who hurt you. You can make yourself treat them with kindness and caring. If you do, you will find that after a while the anger and hurt are gone; almost like they never happened. Then you will begin to know what real forgiveness is.

Being able to forgive others is extremely important if you want to do what pleases God. If you find it hard to give forgiveness, you may want to check out your attitude. A bad attitude will cause you to consider your feelings to be more important and could make you unwilling to forgive. Remember, you should treat others the way you want to be treated, so if you want to be forgiven when you mess up, you should also forgive those who hurt you.

GIVE IT

SOMETIMES WHEN WE HURT others, it seems easier to just act like it never happened rather than ask for forgiveness. We may think that, sooner or later, the person we hurt will get over it and stop being angry. But if we never ask them for forgiveness, they will never know that we're sorry, and they will certainly never know that we will try not to hurt them again. So the person we hurt can never really forget what happened. They will continue to be concerned that we may hurt them again and their fear will cause them to be unable to trust us.

If there is anyone in your life that you have hurt, it's never too late to say you're sorry. Think about all the people in your life. If there is anyone you've hurt or caused problems for, tell them now that you're sorry and will try to never let it happen again. You can write a note or give them a call, but the best way is to look them in the eye. That way they know you mean what you say.

Try it. You'll be amazed how much difference it will make and how wonderful you will feel knowing you did the right thing.

MESSAGE FROM THE *WORD OF PROMISE*

Below you will find a message from Jesus. First find the letters in the grid and then see if you can unscramble the words to discover what Jesus said about forgiveness.

H	F	P	G	L	O	W	U	I	R	A	Y	D	V	N	E	T	B
1	2	3	4	5	6	7	8	9	10	11	12	13	14	15	16	17	18

"...__ __ __ __ __ __ __ __ __ __ __ __ __ __ __ __ __ __
   6 14 2 10 16 4 9   17 10 16 1 6   5 6 3 16 3 16

__ __ __ __ __ __ __ __ __ __ __ __
15 11 13 8 12 6 5 7 9 5 16 18

__ __ __ __ __ __ __ __."
10 9 15 16 14 2 6 4

Unscramble here:

"...__ __ __ __ __ __ __ __ __ __ __ __ __ __ __

__ __ __ __ __ __ __ __ __ __ __

__ __ __ __ __ __ __ __." (Luke 6:37)

Check your answers in the Answer Key at the end of this book

Jesus is forgiveness

To prepare for this session, listen to the **WORD OF PROMISE** New Testament recording of:

Book of Matthew, chapters 9 & 10

Book of Mark, chapters 6

Book of Luke, chapters 9 & 10

When Jesus lived on the earth He was constantly giving to people in need. If someone was sick, He gave them health; if someone was blind, He gave them sight. He fed people who were hungry and gave words of wisdom to everyone. Jesus provided whatever was needed for everyone He met. He didn't want to see anyone in need. In the end, He even gave His life because we all needed a Savior to die in our place and free us from sin and death.

We have already learned that Jesus came to show us how to find a relationship with God and to live in a way that pleases Him. We have discovered the importance of attitude and forgiveness. And we have found out how important it is to always try to think of others first. Now let's take a look at the reason these things are so important. What do they all have in common?

The answer is a simple one—love. Everything that Jesus said and did was because of His deep love for God and for all people. Every choice He made, every action He performed was ruled by love. It was true when He walked the earth and it is just as true now. Jesus loves!

When you're hurting, Jesus cares and wants to help. When life makes you sad, Jesus wants to bring you joy. He cares when things go wrong and will always be there to help if you ask. There will never be a day when He is too busy to spend time with you. And His love is unconditional—there is nothing you can do that will ever cause His love for you to end.

Because of His love for you, Jesus came to earth to show you how to find new, eternal life. That doesn't just mean a new life after you die, but you can have a new life today by following His example. His life was perfect and everything He did was right—everything He did was ruled by love. So if you want to live a successful, new life, love should be at the center of every choice you make.

Jesus Gives

THE GIVING LIST

Change one letter in the first word from the list below to create another word (*pay attention to the hints*). Then change one letter in the new word to discover something that you should be willing to give others. The first one is done for you. **Now see how many you can find.**

GIVE	LIVE	LOVE
BORE	__ ORE	_____
MILE	__ ILE	_____
GOLD	G O __ D	_____
HOLD	H __LD	_____
LISTS	L I __ TS	_____
POLE	__ OLE	_____
TOE	TO__	_____
PLATE	PLA __ E	_____
SLAYER	__LAYER	_____

Check your answers in the Answer Key at the end of this book

Be willing to give

GRAB IT!

Have you ever heard the saying, "Some people are givers, and some people are takers?" It's often said about someone who loves to *receive* things from other people but really hates *giving* anything to anyone. This kind of person is selfish and self-centered. Other people's needs are unimportant to them and they only care about getting their own wants and needs met.

Selfish people don't understand love at all because love is all about giving. It's like selfish people see life in a mirror and loving people see life through a window. If you look in a mirror, you see only yourself. If you look through a window, you see the world outside. What a small, lonely world it is for those who only look in a mirror! And what a wonderfully full world it is for those who look outside.

In order to give love, you have to focus on someone besides yourself. You have to care about what others think and feel. Love is the only thing that exists only if you give it away. If you try to keep it, it isn't love. If you try to save it for later, it will disappear. A poet named Chanh Kha once wrote, "Love isn't love until you give it away." Those are the words of someone who understands the meaning of the real, Jesus kind of love.

HOLD IT!

If you are to follow Jesus' example, you must love others just as He did. Obviously, you can't meet everyone's needs the way He did. Being God's Son gave Him power and authority that you don't have. But it doesn't take power and authority to act lovingly toward others. It only takes a heart that cares about other people and their needs.

There are many needs you can meet if you think about it. You may not be able to heal diseases, but you can visit people who are sick. You may not be able to buy clothes for poor people, but you can give them the ones you don't wear. You can encourage someone who is frightened or give sympathy to someone in pain. If someone is discouraged and depressed, you can give them words of hope. Even something as simple as giving a stranger a smile can be an incredible gift. The smile you gave may be the only good thing that happened to that person all day.

The secret of living a life filled with love is to always look for ways you can give to others. When you do this, an amazing thing happens: you will find making others happy will bring happiness to you. The more you do for others, the more you will enjoy your own life. It's like happiness multiplies when you give it away. And when you give love, it will be given back to you.

Jesus Gives

SAMARITAN SEARCH

Each of these words is found in the story about the Good Samaritan in the tenth chapter of Luke. Locate each word in the grid below. *Remember, they may be spelled diagonally, forward, backward, or upside down.*

Samaritan	Levite	attack
neighbor	robbers	hurt
Jerusalem	road	wounds
priest	sorry	innkeeper
Jericho	beat	money

```
R  O  B  W  O  L  J  B  S  T  M  P  W  X  N
Q  P  K  D  F  H  I  L  N  S  D  N  U  O  W
M  O  N  F  P  D  O  A  E  R  S  Q  M  L  T
M  S  H  F  B  L  O  A  I  E  P  B  Y  J  Q
K  O  W  U  U  Z  U  O  G  B  Y  D  L  B  L
I  N  N  X  R  A  J  F  H  B  K  S  A  E  V
N  C  M  E  B  T  A  E  B  O  R  S  V  M  K
N  U  R  T  Y  T  D  A  O  R  W  I  S  E  D
K  L  O  V  S  A  M  A  R  I  T  A  N  L  E
E  Z  C  J  O  C  N  E  I  E  C  X  W  A  Y
E  L  O  V  R  K  G  I  V  E  L  O  V  S  W
P  O  M  P  R  I  E  S  T  P  R  U  M  U  T
E  V  I  A  Y  R  S  P  V  L  D  T  Q  R  N
R  L  T  I  B  R  Z  X  A  T  L  O  U  E  C
T  O  P  W  K  J  S  J  E  R  I  C  O  J  I
```

Check your answers in the Answer Key at the end of this book

OKAY. Jesus loved everyone and you are to do as He did. So how do you act lovingly toward others everyday? What about when you're upset or having a bad day? How do you give love to other people when you just don't feel like it?

Those are questions every person struggles with. It's really difficult to think about others first when your own life is getting you down. There is no easy answer. It takes determination to act lovingly when you really don't want to. It takes a decision.

Think about the people in your life who give to you nearly everyday: your parents, your family, and your teachers. You can be sure that there are times when their own lives are difficult and it's hard for them to keep on giving to you. But mothers, fathers, teachers, and many others continue to give even when they don't feel like it. Because they care, because they love, they make a decision to do what is best for others instead of pleasing themselves.

The only way you can become a loving, giving person is to make a conscious choice. You have to decide that you will act lovingly, even when you don't feel like it. Real love, a love that doesn't go away during bad times, is based on a decision, not a feeling. Your feelings change constantly. If you don't get enough sleep, you may feel grumpy. If you don't eat right, you may feel tired and depressed. Every minute of every day, something happens that can change how you feel. The only way to become a loving person all the time is to decide to act lovingly because it's the right thing to do, not because you feel like it.

GIVE IT

NOW THAT YOU HAVE a better understanding of what love looks like, try to put it into practice in your life. You could do something as simple as a bit of cleaning for your mom; or you could really give it all you've got and volunteer to mow a lawn or do some other chores for elderly people in your neighborhood.

Take a look around your world (through the window, not in the mirror). Try to find someone with a need you can fulfill. You won't have to look very far.

Remember, you can give love, but you can't keep love. It's only love when you give it away.

Jesus Gives

MESSAGE FROM THE *WORD OF PROMISE*

The grid below contains letters found in a message from Jesus. To discover the right letters for each word, locate the letter on the grid and find the corresponding number, then add 1. The first one is done for you. ***Try to decode the rest of the message to learn what Jesus says about loving others.***

A	B	C	D	E	F	G	H	I	J	K	L	M
1	2	3	4	5	6	7	8	9	10	11	12	13

N	O	P	Q	R	S	T	U	V	W	X	Y	Z
14	15	16	17	18	19	20	21	22	23	24	25	26

"Y o u _ _ _ _ _ _ _ _ _ _ _ _
 x n t   l t r s   k n u d   x n t q

_ _ _ _ _ _ _ _ _ A _ _ _ _ _ _ _ _ _."
m d h f g a n q   r x n t q r d k e
(Luke 10:27)

Check your answers in the Answer Key at the end of this book

 **SESSION SIX: POWER TO LIVE**

To prepare for this session, listen to the **WORD OF PROMISE** New Testament recording of:

Book of Matthew, chapters 11 - 13

Book of Mark, chapters 7 & 8

Book of Luke, chapter 11

Jesus is, without a doubt, the greatest teacher who ever lived. Because He is the Son of God, He knows the truth about all things. Because He lived as a man, He knows exactly what it's like to be human. So when Jesus teaches, we would be wise to listen.

The teachings of Jesus are very different than the kind of teaching most of us are used to. Instead of teaching facts to be memorized or giving formulas to solve problems, Jesus teaches people a whole new way of life. In order to learn to live in God's kingdom we must learn to think differently and respond to life in new ways. Trying to understand things that you've never seen or experienced is extremely difficult, so Jesus often taught in parables. By using stories with deeper meanings, Jesus teaches us how the kingdom of God operates and how we can live successful Christian lives.

de·fine[it]

PARABLE: A parable is a short story that contains a lesson about the right way to think, behave, or believe. It uses a story about something familiar to teach about things that are difficult to understand.

One of the most well-known parables that Jesus taught is about a farmer planting seeds. It seems to be just a lesson on the correct ways to grow crops, but it can teach us a lot about God's kingdom if we understand what it means. To really understand this parable, think of Jesus as the farmer and your life as the soil. All the things He wants to teach you about God's kingdom are the seeds. The plants that grow are all parts of the new life Jesus came to give you.

When a seed is planted, the roots are the first things to grow. A plant that does not have strong roots will soon die. This is just like when Jesus teaches us a truth about God's kingdom. We have to allow that truth to become part of our lives—to let it grow "roots" in our hearts and minds. And then, just like a healthy plant in nature, the strong roots will allow a beautiful plant to grow.

Many things can keep seeds from growing into a healthy plant, just like many things can keep God's truth from really "taking root" and growing in our lives. If the soil of our lives is too hard, we don't allow the truth to grow deeply into our hearts and minds. If we allow the weeds (selfish, sinful attitudes) to remain in our lives, the truth of God will soon find no room to grow. Just as storms can damage plants that are not strong and healthy, if we haven't allowed Jesus' teachings about new life to really take root and grow in our lives, problems and difficult times can cause us to forget what we've learned.

GRAB IT! INTRO

We've taken a look at the parable about the farmer and learned a bit about what it means. Now let's consider the "seeds" we plant in our lives. In this way of thinking, we are the farmer and our lives are the soil. The choices and decisions we make (the "seeds" we plant) will, sooner or later, grow into good or bad results. The whole idea of life being like planting and gathering crops can teach us many things about how to live life as God wants us to.

GRAB IT!

Have you ever had a day when nothing seems to go right? It might go something like this:

You wake up and realize you're running late. You can't find your math book and your homework has disappeared. Because you're late, the bus has already left and your mom gets upset when she has to give you a ride.

You walk in late to class and receive another "tardy" mark against you. Then your missing homework causes you to get a failing grade for the day.

It seems the day just keeps going from bad to worse until, at the end of the day, you find yourself angry at the world and feeling sorry for yourself. So you close yourself up in your room and just wait for tomorrow to come.

Days like this happen to everyone. The secret of dealing with them is in making the right choices, even when things are not going your way. If you make wrong choices in the way you handle problems today, chances are pretty good you will find trouble waiting for you tomorrow.

Just like a seed will only grow the kind of plant it came from, our bad decisions will cause negative things to happen, and our good choices will bring about positive results. It's like we plant our choices and they grow into something that is exactly like what we planted.

All the things that happened on the bad day described above could have been avoided if good choices had been made the day before. (Set an alarm clock and get up when it rings. Then you won't be late. If you always put things where they belong, they won't get lost.) But because bad seeds were planted, bad things grew.

Even when bad choices have created a whole crop of bad things, you still have the ability to keep the situation from getting worse. You just need to admit you're the one who messed up and apologize for your bad choices. Then you start over and decide to do better next time. If you learn from your mistakes, it will keep you from planting those bad seeds again.

WHAT WILL GROW?

The two columns below contain synonyms (words that mean nearly the same thing). See if you can connect the words that have similar meanings. Remember: whatever you plant is the crop that will grow.

If you plant:	You will grow:
Responsibility	Hopefulness
Happiness	Lying
Truthfulness	Self-centeredness
Joy	Gloominess
Peace	Honesty
Anger	Rage
Selfishness	Harmony
Dishonesty	Cheerfulness
Negative thinking	Reliability
Positive thinking	Delight

Check your answers in the Answer Key at the end of this book

HOLD IT!

There are many ways to find good seeds to plant in our lives. The most important is by discovering all the things that Jesus taught and how He lived His life on earth. If we follow His example, our lives can grow huge crops of the things that please God. Let's take a look at some of them.

JESUS KNEW THE BIBLE.

Jesus studied the Bible and even memorized it. He knew that everything in the Bible is true, because even though it was written by men, God told them exactly what to write. He could live His life exactly the way God wanted because He knew all the truth of God's Word.

JESUS WAS A GOOD FRIEND.

Jesus never thought of Himself first. He was constantly watching to see what He could do to help others. He cried with those who were sad and always had time to listen whenever someone needed to talk about their lives.

JESUS WAS A GOOD SON.

Jesus loved His mother and was always an obedient son. When He got older, He took care of Mary and provided for all her needs. Before He died, He asked His best friend, John, to take care of her and treat her like his own mother.

JESUS ALWAYS SPOKE THE TRUTH.

No matter the situation, Jesus never lied. He knew that lying is against God's rules because lying will always end up hurting someone—either the liar or someone else. We can believe everything Jesus said because He never said anything that was not true.

JESUS LOVED GOD.

Jesus enjoyed spending time with God, so He talked to God often. Because He loved God, Jesus wanted to know how to live His life in the way that would please God. Love always considers the wants and needs of someone else first, and Jesus cared deeply about what God wanted and always did exactly what God told Him to do.

Those are just some of the good seeds that can be planted in your life. But you have to make sure you take care of the soil (your heart and mind). You have to be willing to learn and ready to make right decisions. If you do, your life will be filled with the best crop—living life in the way that pleases God.

WORD GAME

SUCCESSFUL FARMING

Think about all the things Jesus said and did in the parts of the New Testament you have listened to so far. See how many other "good seeds" you can find. Write the name of the seed on the first line. On the second line, tell what might grow from the "seed." The first one is done for you.

Seed: _Jesus attended church services._

What will grow? _If we attend church services, we learn about God's_ kingdom and how to live our lives in a way that pleases God.

Seed: _____

What will grow? _____

_____

_____

Seed _____

What will grow? _____

_____

_____

.

WE'VE LOOKED AT HOW GOD plants seeds in your life. God plants only good seeds, but whether they grow well is up to you.

We've also talked about the seeds you plant into your own life. Whether they are good or bad is your choice. Whatever you plant is what you will allow to grow in your life.

Both God's seeds and the good seeds you plant need proper soil in which to grow. Good soil is soft and fertile (filled with all the good things plants need to grow). Rocks must be removed and weeds pulled up if healthy plants are to grow.

So you must take good care of the soil of your life (your heart and your mind). Make sure to keep your mind ready to learn about God's plan for your life. Read the Bible and listen to God's voice so your mind will be filled with His truth. Keep it focused on good things and never allow the weeds of sinful thoughts to grow. Be careful to keep a good attitude toward others and have a heart that is ready to love and give. A negative attitude will cause your heart to be hard and cold, just like a stone.

If you make sure your heart and mind are like good soil, all the seeds that God plants will grow and become healthy in your life. Then making right choices and keeping your attitude right will become so much easier. The more of God's seeds that grow up in your heart and mind, the more good seeds you will have to plant in your life.

GIVE IT

One really great way of keeping your heart and mind healthy and ready to become good soil for the seeds God plants is to memorize Jesus' words. It's amazing how the things Jesus said will help when you have a decision to make or when life gets difficult.

In an earlier session, you listened to the "Beatitudes" Jesus taught. This is a very important sermon that can help you live a life that pleases God. The Beatitudes sermon is printed below. Keep reading it until you have it memorized. It may seem difficult at first, but if you take the time, you will find Jesus' words contain answers, direction, and incredible wisdom. The truths contained in these few words can make your life incredibly rich soil for the seeds of God's truth that Jesus will plant in your life.

> "Those people who know they have great spiritual needs are happy. The kingdom of heaven belongs to them. Those who are sad now are happy. God will comfort them. Those who are humble are happy. The earth will belong to them. Those who want to do right more than anything else are happy. God will fully satisfy

them. Those who give mercy to others are happy. Mercy will be given to them. Those who are pure in their thinking are happy. They will be with God. Those who work to bring peace are happy. God will call them his sons. Those who are treated badly for doing good are happy. The kingdom of heaven belongs to them." (Matthew 5:3–10)

WORD GAME

MESSAGE FROM THE *WORD OF PROMISE*

The message from Jesus below contains words that are in code. The alphabet has been scrambled and each letter actually stands for another letter (for example: A=c and S=f). To break the code try to discover the letter that should have been used. Some letters have been decoded for you. *Hint: As you discover the right letter, write it into the grid.*

A	B	C	D	E	F	G	H	I	J	K	L	M
	g	n		v	l			s	y		r	

N	O	P	Q	R	S	T	U	V	W	X	Y	Z
e		t	z				m		k	q	b	

"B U T W H _ _ I _ _ _ _ E _ _ _ _ _ _ _ _
 p d w u a c w o f w a j f j j n w a c w

_ _ _ _ O _ _ _ _ _ _ _ _ _ R _ _ _ _?
v j h h x e w a j l x x n l i x d e n

_ _ _ _ _ _ _ _ L _ _ _ _ _ _ _
w a c w f j j n o f h o y j w a j

_ _ R _ _ _ W H O _ _ _ _ _ _ _
t j i f x e u a x a j c i f w a j

_ _ _ _ _ _ _ _ _ _ _ U N D E R S T A N D S
w j c g a o e l c e n d e n j i f w c e n f

_ _." (Matthew 13:23)
o w

Check your answers in the Answer Key at the end of this book

To prepare for this session, listen to the *WORD OF PROMISE* New Testament recording of:

Book of Matthew, chapters 14 -16

Book of Mark, chapter 9

Book of Luke, chapter 12

Get It! SESSION SEVEN: TO THOSE WHO SEEK

Everyone is seeking a successful life. The only difference is the way each person defines success. For some it means money, power, or fame. Others think success means being popular and having countless friends.

Commercials and advertisements can make us think we need to find the perfect look or the perfect life in order to find success. They tell us things like:

"Buy this cream and you will look great. Everyone will envy you!"

"Use our computer program and you'll get better grades than anyone else!"

"If you want to be popular in school, buy the clothes from our store!"

Those words can make us think that success means being smarter, more popular, more attractive, or just *better than* everyone else. According to the voices in commercials, we must own the best things, have the most friends, end up with the most glamorous, well-paying job, and have nothing but fun all day, in order to be successful. The world tries to tell us success is all about circumstances (the things, activities, and people in our lives).

The truth is that most people live average lives. They have friends, but are not among the most popular people; they live in average homes with enough money to buy the things they need. Most people have opportunities to relax and have fun, but duties and responsibilities must come first. Few people are famous, or the smartest, or the best-looking.

Even those who do have all the things the world calls important (money, good looks, fame, power) can be convinced that they must keep seeking more and more. Otherwise, they could end up less successful than someone who has acquired more things than they have.

If people seek wealth, they will spend their lives trying to get it. If they seek fame, power, or the "perfect" life, the search will never end. Someone else will always have more.

So how does anyone find success?

The things the world considers important will never bring true success. The world's kind of success will always be something we keep chasing but never catch. True success is not about the things in your life. It's all about how you live your life.

True success is eternal and available to everyone.

GRAB IT!

When we are born again, we actually become citizens of God's kingdom. His kingdom is totally different than the world so we have to learn a new way to live. Jesus came to teach us how to live as citizens of the kingdom of God.

In the "Hear It" section of this session, you heard Jesus tell you not to be concerned with acquiring things; not even food or clothing. He wants you to understand that the circumstances of life shouldn't be most important. Instead, what you should want most is "the kingdom of God."

de·fine [it]

GLORY This word means honor; respect, and love. When we give glory to God we cause others to realize that God is good. He is deserving of all the love and respect we have to give.

To understand those words, you must realize that the kingdom of God is more than a place. It's also a way of thinking and behaving that brings glory to God. As a citizen of God's kingdom, you should live now in the same way you will live when you are taken to heaven. God should rule your life now just as He will then.

There are two rules (or commandments) in God's kingdom that are more important than all others:

1. Love God.

2. Love others as yourself.

If you follow those commandments, you will always bring glory to God. Others will always be able to see what God is like by looking at you. That's because God is love. God doesn't just have love or give love, but God *is* love.

So in God's kingdom, love is the most important thing. The way you treat others is infinitely more important than the circumstances of your life. Instead of trying to make your own life better, in God's kingdom you should think of others first. Rather than seeking money, or power, or fame, you should seek to live your life as a citizen of God's kingdom. Don't try to acquire things to be successful, give love away and find true success.

Let's take a look at how that works.

But first . . .

WORD GAME

WORDS OF LOVE

Within this game there are 20 words associated with love. Locate and circle as many as you can find from the list below. Remember, they may go up, down, across, backward or diagonally. *See if you can find all 20.*

```
R E S O R M D L P A T I E N C E
E M Q C A R E B W V I C A P Z M
S O P S O U L M R J O H O N O R
P D T G H M L F Y J V I S S E S
E G X O K E M J M Q E R W O T K
C N U F Y R D A L C N S B P K H
T I T D R J R S N N M O U D I T
W K C P O U M D X D K U Y S N S
C Y D R L O Q Z W L M I R N D E
H D O O G Y B T M L D E L M N T
O R N I G O D I S R X U N O E A
O O A D N T U M D I D L A T S E
S S B L Z H O S U N N I P R S R
E E G I V E M R X B I L N U D G
U T I L W R A P O S C M O S B W
H E A R T S S E L D N E A T Z Q
```

GIVE	RESPECT	GLORY
CARE	GOD	HEART
HONOR	OTHERS	MIND
TRUST	YOU	COMMANDMENT
CHOOSE	ENDLESS	GOOD
PATIENCE	JESUS	GREATEST
KINDNESS	KINGDOM	

Check your answers in the Answer Key at the end of this book

HOLD IT!

People who seek good circumstances in life end up finding things that can either be lost or ruined. People lose fame, money, and power everyday. Everything you can buy will one day wear out and become nothing but garbage. You can be popular one day and lose dozens of friends the next. The circumstances of life change constantly; and everything the world has to offer will one day come to an end.

So why spend your time seeking something that will only be lost? Seems pointless, doesn't it?

Things in God's kingdom never end—they are eternal. You are a citizen of that kingdom. Instead of seeking the things in the world that will end, set out to find the things that will last forever: living right with God, peace, and joy.

If you seek to live right with God, you will always consider Him and others before yourself. This way of living is called "righteousness." Since God is love, in order to live the way He wants, you must always choose to be loving.

de•fine[it]

RIGHTEOUSNESS: When we believe in Jesus and accept the new life He brings, we become able to leave sinful attitudes and actions behind. We are then free to live a life that pleases God. The ability to live in a right way because of Jesus is called "righteousness."

Most people understand the word "peace" to be the lack of arguments and fighting. And it's true that loving others can cause those things to end. But peace in God's kingdom is more than peaceful circumstances; it's a calm, trusting heart that knows God is in control. If you know that God is love, it's easy to trust Him to do only what is good for you. And that will fill your heart with peace.

We've already learned that joy is a kind of happiness that comes from inside, no matter what's happening in the world around you. Joy causes a positive attitude that makes it easier to make the choices that please God. The choices that please God are always ruled by love.

It's obvious that love is the most important thing in the kingdom of God. Because you are a citizen of that kingdom, a life that gives love freely is what you should be seeking. If you seek to be loving, then you seek God and the best for all His people. If you live a life guided by love, you will always please God and find peace and joy in your life. Seeking to give love at all times will always bring positive results (though you may not always see them right away); and positive results lead to a successful life.

FIND SUCCESS

The word "success" is hidden 10 times in the grid below. Can you find them all? Remember, the word may be written up, down, backward, forward, or diagonally.

S	S	U	C	S	U	C	C	E	S	S
S	U	C	S	U	S	C	E	S	U	U
E	C	C	U	C	S	E	C	U	S	C
S	S	E	C	C	U	S	S	C	S	C
U	S	E	C	E	S	S	U	C	E	E
C	E	C	E	S	S	E	C	C	U	S
C	C	U	S	S	U	S	E	S	C	S
E	U	E	S	S	E	C	C	U	S	U
S	E	S	U	C	C	E	S	S	S	E
S	S	S	E	S	S	E	C	C	U	S
E	S	U	C	C	E	S	S	C	S	S

Check your answers in the Answer Key at the end of this book

LIVE IT!

JESUS' WORDS AND THE WAY HE LIVED His life will lead you to find the things of God's kingdom. Everything He said and everything He did pleased God. If you read the Bible and learn His words, you will learn how to live as He did.

We learned earlier about the good "seeds" God sows in our lives. The words of Jesus are like seeds filled with all those good things. Once those seeds grow into healthy plants, fruit will begin to grow. Each piece of fruit is one of the eternal things God wants to bring into our lives; the "fruit" of living right with God with peace and joy in our hearts.

If fruit is never picked, it never does anyone any good. It has to be picked and eaten to have any purpose at all. But if we eat it, it becomes a part of us and gives us health and strength to continue living. So it is with the fruit that God grows in our lives; if we never use it, it won't ever become a part of our lives.

Fill your heart and mind with the words of Jesus and learn God's truth. Then the good fruit of right living with God will grow in your life. Look inside your heart and mind for that fruit and listen to the voice inside that leads you to do what is right. When you do what pleases God, you are living your life in His kingdom. That's where you'll find true success—the kind that never ends.

GIVE IT

IMAGINE YOUR FRIEND'S PARENTS are going away for the evening and your friend decides to have a party while they're gone. All the popular kids will be there and you really want to go; but you know your parents won't let you attend parties without supervision. What do you do?

You could decide not to tell your mom and dad that your friend's parents aren't home (after all, they may never find out), or you could decide not to go. The choice is yours.

If you seek the things of God's kingdom, you will seek the right way. In order to make the right choice, you must ask yourself what Jesus would want you to do. Choosing the right way can be very difficult and it can mean saying "no" to things you really want to do. But, remember, God's kingdom is not about circumstances, it's about a way of life.

Instead of seeking fun for a few hours at the risk of losing your parents' trust, you can decide to seek the eternal things: right living with God, peace, and joy. Instead of seeking to make yourself most important, you should consider God and your parents first. If you always let love guide your choices, and use the good fruit that God is growing in your life, you will always live a life that pleases God. That is the true definition of success.

MESSAGE FROM THE *WORD OF PROMISE*

The words below are written in code. To find the right letters, use the code key.
Then put the words in the right order to discover the message from Jesus.

bpfo = W H A T

opc = T H E

bfaok = W A N T S

ngy = Y O U

ugko = M O S T

fal = A N D

opmar = T H I N G

bfao = W A N T

lgmar = D O I N G

mk = I S

emarlgu = K I N G D O M

kpgyvl = S H O U L D

Code Key

A	B	C	D	E	F	G	H	I	J	K	L	M
f	x	j	l	c	h	r	p	m	z	e	v	u

N	O	P	Q	R	S	T	U	V	W	X	Y	Z
a	g	s	d	t	k	o	y	q	b	i	n	w

"THE THING YOU SHOULD WANT

MOST IS GOD'S KINGDOM AND

DOING WHAT GOD WANTS." (Matthew 6:33)

Check your answers in the Answer Key at the end of this book

To prepare for this session, listen to the **WORD OF PROMISE** New Testament recording of:

Book of Matthew, chapters 17-18

Book of Mark, chapter 10

Book of Luke, chapters 13-14

 **SESSION EIGHT: TO LIVE GOD'S WAY**

Being young can really be difficult. It may seem that someone is always telling you what to do. Someone else decides where you live, what you're allowed to do, and where you're allowed to go. You have to ask permission before you make plans, and you often hear "no" when you'd rather hear "yes." If you don't do as adults tell you, your disobedience can bring you trouble.

You may look at adults and think their lives are so much better than your own. They are free to do what they want, and they are free to go wherever they choose. You probably can't wait until you are grown and are free to make your own decisions. Then your life will be your own and no one can tell you what to do. How awesome will that be? Life as an adult must be a lot better, right?

So if being an adult is so great, why did Jesus say that the kingdom of God belongs to those people who are like little children? Why would Jesus want all of us to be like little kids?

Let's take a look at some differences between kids and adults.

People your age have responsibilities at school and at home. You have to attend school every day, pay attention in class, and follow the rules. At home you may have chores, homework, little brothers and sisters to look after, and more rules to follow. As you get older, your life gets filled up with more and more activities and responsibilities. As you learn to do more things and handle more responsibility, life will get busier and more difficult. One day you will be an adult and all the choices and responsibilities for your life will be yours.

Growing up to the point where you can handle greater responsibility and make your own decisions is not a bad thing. But as people become able to handle life on their own, they can sometimes forget that God is the One in control. Older people, especially adults, can begin to think they can handle life on their own and don't need anyone's help.

Being able to handle responsibilities and make your own choices can make you think you have nothing else to learn. Whenever anyone, no matter what age, thinks that they don't need God's help to live their lives in the right way, they will end up making wrong choices and making a mess of things.

Little children know they need help to learn how to live.

GRAB IT!

Babies learn that they can walk by watching older people. But no matter how often they see someone walk, they have no idea how to do it themselves. They have to be taught. At first someone must hold them up and walk along with them to show them how. After a lot of practice (and a lot of falling), a baby will soon learn to walk on its own.

Can you imagine how strange it would be for a baby to say, "I don't want you to teach me?" Of course babies can't talk, but they might just refuse to try walking or give up the first time they fall. Either way, they would never learn.

Since nearly everyone learns to walk, it's obvious that babies are great at learning. They listen closely and try to do as older people tell them. They trust that older people know the right way to keep them safe as they try to learn. But most of all, babies want to learn.

In the "Hear It" section of this lesson, Jesus tells us that we should be like little children. He wants us to understand that we should be ready and willing to learn. We should be like the baby learning to walk—we should listen closely to Jesus' words, realize He will teach us the right things that will please God, and trust that He will always do what is best for us.

Learning how to walk is much like learning how to live in God's kingdom. If we want to grow up in God's kingdom we must learn to get from where we are to where we want to be. Just like in walking when we take one step at a time, we need to keep moving forward in our lives in God's kingdom. We move forward by believing Jesus' words, listening to God's voice, and by making the right choices. Jesus will teach us the way a citizen of God's kingdom should walk.

FOLLOWING DIRECTIONS

The grid below contains all the letters needed to discover something about little children. *Follow the directions to locate the right words.* Then put the words in the right order to solve the puzzle.

Baby	Willing	Jesus	Walk	Learn	Humble
Trust	Truth	Live	Try	Taught	Practice
Learn	Listen	From	Little	Ready	Help
Choices	Believe	People	Child	And	Kids
Teach	Be	Please	Agree	Small	Children
Are	Loving	Always	Realize	What	You
Don't	Know	To	Live	Life	Right

	Direction	Write the word here.
1.	Start with the word in Blue.	— — — — — —
2.	Count down 4 spaces and left 1 space.	— —
3.	Count up 2 spaces and right 3 spaces.	— — — — — — — —
4.	Count up 2 spaces and left 5 spaces.	— — — — —
5.	Count up 2 spaces and right 1 space.	— — — — — — —
6.	Count down 5 spaces and left 1 space.	— — —
7.	Count up 2 spaces and right 4 spaces.	— — —
8.	Count up 3 spaces and right 1 space.	— — — — — —

Little _____ _____ _____ _____

_____ _____ _____.

Check your answers in the Answer Key at the end of this book

HOLD IT!

"Little children are humble." What exactly does that mean?

Someone who is humble realizes their own limitations. They know the things they can do and the things they can't. A humble person knows that other people are necessary in their lives to teach them and help them live the right way. A humble person is always ready to learn and receive truth. And a humble person is always ready to give when someone else is in need.

Pride is the opposite of humility.

People who are prideful refuse to listen to others or to admit they need to learn. They think they always know what's best and won't allow anyone to teach them anything.

When someone is born into God's kingdom and becomes a Christian, they are like a baby. They need to learn all the things necessary to live their lives. Jesus tells us that we should be humble like little children so that we will realize we have a lot to learn and be willing to have Him teach us a new way of life—the life in God's kingdom.

If you want to do as Jesus said and become like a little child, take a look at your life. Do you realize and admit that you still have things to learn? Are you willing to listen to others and let them teach you?

Really listen to Jesus' words and believe what He says. Try to make humility a part of your life. Then you will live like a citizen of God's kingdom should and your life will bring glory to God.

YOU HAVE ALREADY LEARNED some very important things and you even make some of your own choices. There are things you do well and some abilities you have that others may not. You may have nice hair or an attractive face. You may be good at sports or get good grades. It's not wrong to admit the things you know, or what you do well, or any of the good things about you. Everyone should have positive feelings about themselves. There's only one you, and you should be the best you can be.

The problem comes when you begin to think you have nothing more to learn and no one is quite as good or important as you. That kind of thinking is prideful and conceited. It will cause you to be difficult to get along with and bring all sorts of trouble into your life.

People who are prideful and conceited usually demand their own way and refuse to listen to anyone else. These people have a hard time accepting that they have not learned everything and they don't have all the answers. When people have pride in their hearts, they consider their wants and ideas as better and more important; they think they need no one's help. Prideful people live selfish lives and rarely think of others.

It's easy to tell which people are humble and which people are prideful by the way they respond to people and circumstances.

Humble people don't consider themselves most important so they think of others first.

Prideful people think they are more important than anyone else, so they always want things their way.

Humble people are happy for others when good things happen for them.

Prideful people would rather all good things happen only for themselves.

Humble people realize they don't know all things, so they listen and learn.

Prideful people always think they know best, so they refuse to listen and are difficult to teach.

Take a good look at the way you respond to other people. Is there pride or humility in your heart?

PRIDE OR HUMILITY

When your parents try to explain why you are not allowed to do something, how do you respond? _____

_____

How would a humble person respond? _____

_____

If you are in a class at school that you don't like, how do you act in the class? _____

_____

How would a humble person choose to behave? _____

_____

If you really want to go to a football game, but your friend wants to watch a movie instead, what do you do? _____

_____

What is the humble response? _____

_____

When a friend gets a gift and it's something you really want, how do you feel?

_____

_____

How would a humble person react? _____

_____

So how did you do? Which is in your heart, pridefulness or humility?

GIVE IT

NO MATTER HOW YOU ANSWERED the questions above, don't feel bad about yourself. Everyone struggles with being humble, it's not an easy choice. But it is the best choice.

If there are areas in your life that are prideful, just tell Jesus you are sorry and want to change. He will forgive you as soon as you ask and then, if you listen, He will teach you how to think and act with humility.

Try to spend an entire day trying to make choices with a humble heart. Think of others first and realize you have a lot to learn. Everyone in your life will be happy you did and you will end up making yourself happy, too.

Once you decide to be humble like a little child, you will have made a huge step toward learning to walk the right way in the kingdom of God.

Try to make choices with a humble heart.

MESSAGE FROM THE *WORD OF PROMISE*

The words below are written in code. To find the right letters, use the code key. **Then put the words in the right order to discover the message from Jesus.** (Hint: one word is used three times.)

sctkga = P E R S O N

poc = __ __ __

ocxqca = __ __ __ __ __ __

gac = __ __ __

vmec = __ __ __ __

bog = __ __ __

mk = __ __

uxeck = __ __ __ __ __

pomk = __ __ __ __

jomvl = __ __ __ __ __

gh = __ __

omukcvh = __ __ __ __ __ __ __

ma = __ __

emarlgu = __ __ __ __ __ __ __

Code Key

A	B	C	D	E	F	G	H	I	J	K	L	M
x	f	j	l	c	h	r	o	m	z	e	v	u

N	O	P	Q	R	S	T	U	V	W	X	Y	Z
a	g	s	d	y	k	p	y	q	b	n	n	w

"__ __ __ GREATEST __ __ __ __ __ __ __ __ __ __ __ __

__ __ __ __ __ __ __ __ __ __ __ __ __ __ __ __ __ __ __ __

__ __ __ __ __ __ __ __ __ __ __ __ __ __ __ __ __ __ HUMBLE

__ __ __ __ __ __ __ __ CHILD." (Matthew 18:4)

Check your answers in the Answer Key at the end of this book

 SESSION NINE: **GOD'S SON**

To prepare for this session, listen to the **WORD OF PROMISE** New Testament recording of:

Book of Matthew, chapters 19-20

Book of Mark, chapter 11

Book of Luke, chapters 15-17

It seems few days go by that we don't hear on the news about another child who has been abducted. Some evil person has convinced a child to come with them and has taken them away into danger.

Kidnapping is one of the most incredibly wicked crimes because innocent children are put in danger. Can you imagine how horrible it is for a little child when a cruel stranger takes them away from home? Imagine how frightened and alone they feel.

As horrible as it is for the child, the parents' suffering is just as great. They warned their child about the danger of following a stranger, but the child didn't listen. Now their child is gone. Their hearts are broken and they live in fear that something will happen to the little one they love so much. They are willing to do absolutely anything to see their child out of danger and safely at home again; they are willing to give all they have, even their lives.

Did you know the entire world has been kidnapped? Everyone who lives has been taken away from home and into danger by a cruel stranger.

Here's the story:

Remember the garden where Adam and Eve first lived? It was a wonderful place filled with all they could ever want. They understood that God was their Father and they knew He would always take care of them.

Then Satan came, and like a cruel kidnapper, convinced Adam and Eve to do as he wanted. Because they chose to listen to Satan instead of God, their Father, they were taken away from their home and taken to Satan's kingdom. There they found themselves surrounded by sickness, pain, and death—the penalties for sin.

Adam and Eve were kidnapped and taken into sin—Satan's kingdom. All people born after them—all God's children—are born in the same place. Before we know Jesus, we are like little children who are lost and frightened and in the hands of a cruel stranger.

But our Father will do anything to see us out of danger and safely home again!

GRAB IT!

When a child has been kidnapped, they are powerless to help themselves. They can't get away without help. Someone must care enough to defeat the kidnapper and free the child from danger. Someone must clear the way for the child to return home. Someone must come to their rescue.

A rescuer is someone who will do anything necessary to save another person. Rather than think of themselves, they consider only the need of the person in trouble. They are even willing to give their lives to bring someone else to safety.

Think back to the first session in this book. We learned that Jesus is our Savior. Savior means someone who rescues another from danger. God saw that His children were kidnapped into Satan's kingdom and trapped by the power of sin. So He sent a Rescuer—He sent Jesus to defeat Satan and make a way for us to return home to our Father.

Because of Jesus' love for you, He has rescued you from the power of sin. Jesus defeated Satan and gave His life to set you free. You only need to accept and believe that Jesus died to free you from Satan's kingdom. Then you can choose to walk away from the dangers of sin.

Jesus' love rescues you from the power of sin.

GOD'S KINGDOM

SATAN'S KINGDOM

God's Son

Check your answers in the Answer Key at the end of this book

HOLD IT!

Every kingdom has a ruler. Satan rules his kingdom—the kingdom of sickness, sin, and death. But when people are born again, they become a part of God's kingdom and God is their Ruler. Satan has no right to rule over them. He no longer has them kidnapped and in his power.

God is the ruler over the people in His kingdom. But Satan still wants to convince you to disobey God. He will try to make you choose things that are against God's rules and things that will end up hurting you. That is called temptation. Satan will always try to convince people that sinful attitudes and actions will make them happy. He will lie to you and try to cause you to make wrong choices and disobey God's rules.

Because God loves you, He will not force you to make right choices and follow His rules; He leaves it up to you. He doesn't want you to obey Him because you have to; He wants you to choose to obey. If you had no choice, then your obedience wouldn't really come from your own heart. If someone forces you to obey, then obedience is really their decision, not yours.

The choice is up to you. You can realize that Jesus has rescued you from Satan's kingdom and choose to do as God wants, or you can act like you are still kidnapped by Satan and allow him to cause you to make choices that displease God.

LIVE IT!

When we fail to do what pleases God and live like we are still kidnapped into Satan's kingdom, we have sinned. When we sin, God feels just like the parents of a child who has been stolen from home. He is heartbroken and concerned for our safety.

In the "Hear It" section of this chapter, you heard a story about a son who took all his father gave him and left home. The son made many bad choices and lost everything. Just like the father in the story, God will let us make wrong choices if that is our decision. He will not force us to stay with Him where we are safe. He will let us take all the good things He has given us and waste them if we want. He allows us to live our lives in any way we choose.

But there is never a time when God forgets about us or gives up on us. God will always keep hoping we return home and will never stop loving us. His love is unconditional—it will never end regardless of what happens.

Jesus gave His life to set us free. When we realize we have done wrong and made a mess of our lives, we only need to repent—make the choice to not be ruled by sin, realize we are free, ask to be forgiven, and go back home. God will not be waiting to tell us how horrible we've been, but He will be waiting to see our face and welcome us back into safety. The moment He sees us, He will run to meet us with incredible love and acceptance. Just like the parents of a kidnapped child, He will be overjoyed when His child returns.

GIVE IT

Whenever someone is born again, they have chosen to walk away from the place of sin and death and are free to live in God's kingdom.

Everyone you know who is not a Christian is still being held by Satan. They are still kidnapped and in danger. But now you know that Jesus defeated Satan and cleared the way for them to be free.

Telling other people about Jesus and what He has done for them can be difficult. You may be concerned that they will laugh at you or think you're weird. But most people really want to know the truth.

Try telling your family about how Jesus saved them from Satan's kingdom. You know the people you love care about what you have to say. Then you may find it easier to tell your friends about the new life they can have through Jesus.

There is no gift you could give that will ever mean as much. Knowing Jesus died to set you free is the greatest gift on earth.

WORD GAME

MESSAGE FROM THE *WORD OF PROMISE*

Locate the correct letter in the grid and write it in the space provided. Then use the second set of spaces to unscramble the words. *See if you can discover what Jesus said about the reason for His life.*

H	F	P	G	L	O	M	C	I	R
1	2	3	4	5	6	7	8	9	10

A	Y	D	V	N	E	T	B	S
11	12	13	14	15	16	17	18	19

" _ _ _   _ _ _   _ _   _ _ _   _ _ _ _   _ _

  16 17 1   15 19 6   2 6   11 15 7   7 8 16 11   6 17

_ _ _ _   _ _ _   _ _ _ _   _ _   _ _ _ _   _ _ _ _

14 16 4 9   9 19 1   2 16 9 5   6 17   11 19 16 14   11 12 7 15

_ _ _ _ _ _." (Matthew 20:28)

16 16 5 6 3 3

Unscramble here:

"..._ _ _   _ _ _   _ _   _ _ _   _ _ _ _   _ _

_ _ _   _ _ _   _ _ _ _   _ _   _ _ _ _   _ _ _ _

_ _ _ _ _ _." (Matthew 20:28)

To check your answers, turn to the Answer Key at the end of this book.

To prepare for this session, listen to the *WORD OF PROMISE* New Testament recording of:

Book of Matthew, chapters 21-23

Book of Luke, chapters 18-20

You have already learned many things about Jesus. You know that Jesus' death paid the ransom to free you from Satan's kingdom and the power of sin. You have learned how to become a citizen in God's kingdom. You know Jesus' life and words will teach you how to live in that kingdom. And you know that the choice to live a life that pleases God is totally up to you.

Now it's time to learn the rest of the story.

We have already learned that a death had to happen for people to be set free from Satan's kingdom and reconnected to God. Before Jesus was born, God provided a way for people to be connected to Him for short periods of time by having them sacrifice a lamb. The lamb had to be absolutely perfect. It could have no spots or defects of any kind. The death of this perfect animal paid the penalty for sin, but only for a short time.

de·fine [*it*]

SACRIFICE: This word means to give something precious. In the Bible, sacrifice means to kill something in order to give it to God.

Back in the days before Jesus was born, the animals people owned were extremely important to them. There were no grocery stores, so the animals were the only meat people had to eat. Instead of using money to pay for things, people back then often traded an animal for other things they needed. When God told them to kill an animal, it was no small thing.

When an animal was sacrificed to God, it was as if the animal killed had absorbed all the sin of the people. It was as though the animal carried the sins of the people inside itself. (Think how a sponge absorbs water and then holds it inside.) When the animal died, the sin was taken away and the people were able to be reconnected to God, but only for one year.

de·fine [*it*]

ALTAR: A place set aside for the worship of God. An altar is usually a structure of some sort, like a table or a raised platform. In the Bible, it was often a pile of rock or stone.

Once the animal was killed, the blood from the animal was taken and sprinkled on an altar. In God's eyes, the sprinkled blood covered the sinful acts and attitudes of the people. God saw only the blood, not the sin.

All this may seem very strange. We don't do things like this anymore. But to the people who lived long ago, this was just a normal part of life. They understood it. The ones who wanted to be reconnected to God always made sure they sacrificed an animal to Him once a year. That way, the sin that separated them from God was gone and the sinful acts they committed were covered over by the blood of the animal. They could be reconnected to God and He would not see their sinful actions and attitudes, but only for one year at a time.

HOLIDAYS

Did you know the word "holiday" used to be "holy day?" Long ago, the only days that were set aside as special were days when people worshiped God in a special way. One of those days was the day the animal was sacrificed to God. That day was called "The Day of Atonement." In the Bible, the word "atone" means to make peace. It also can mean to cover something or clean something. Below you will find the definitions of some holidays we celebrate today. *See if you can match the holiday to the correct definition.* You will find the list of holidays at the end of the list of definitions.

1. This is the day we celebrate Jesus' birth. Since we are not sure exactly which day He was born, this is the day we remember that God sent His Son to be born as a man for us.

HOLIDAY:_____

2. This is the day we remember that Jesus rose from the dead. We haven't talked about that yet, but Jesus' death was not the end. He actually came back to life and walked out of His grave!

HOLIDAY: _____

3. This is the day we remember all the things that God has done for us. It's a day for spending time with the people we love and thanking God for all we have.

HOLIDAY: _____

Holiday used to be "Holy Day."

4. This day is set aside to tell people we love that they are special to us. But every day is a good day for that, right?

HOLIDAY: _____

5. This is a holiday that some people don't actually celebrate. You may never have heard about it. But this is a very important day for God's kingdom. It's the day He sent the Holy Spirit to help people live their lives in the way that pleases God.

HOLIDAY: _____

6. This is a day to remember all the people who fought in the wars and may have even sacrificed their lives so that we can live as free people in the United States.

HOLIDAY: _____

7. This is the day we remember the people who work hard everyday to provide the things we need. Like our parents, who sacrifice their time to work and give us better lives.

HOLIDAY: _____

HOLIDAYS: Memorial Day, Pentecost, Christmas, Labor Day, Valentine's Day, Easter

Check your answers in the Answer Key at the end of this book

GRAB IT!

When Jesus was born, God had a plan. He didn't want people to have to sacrifice animals every year in order to be connected to Him. He wanted everyone to be able to know Him and be a part of His kingdom, constantly and forever. So He sent Jesus to be the final sacrifice. Jesus came to do the same thing that the sacrificed animal used to do—reconnect people with God and cover their sins with His blood.

Here's how it happened:

Jesus is God's Son—the Messiah. He understands all the things about God and His kingdom. There is no sin in Him and He never fails to do exactly what pleases God. Jesus is perfect.

All these things were true when Jesus lived on earth as a man. And these are the very things that made Jesus' enemies extremely angry. They realized Jesus knew more than they did and they were concerned that people would no longer listen to them. And when Jesus told them He was God's Son, they were filled with rage. They couldn't understand how this poor carpenter could be the Son of God. They expected the Messiah to be powerful and impressive. They believed Jesus had to be a dangerous liar.

They soon decided that the only way to make sure that Jesus did not continue to teach and claim to be God's Son was to put Him to death. And they did.

Jesus had never done anything but love others and help anyone in need. He had never sinned—never one time in His entire life. But He was sentenced to die in the same way robbers and murderers were put to death. They decided to kill Jesus by nailing Him to a cross.

Before Jesus was nailed to a cross, He was beaten by soldiers and they spit in His face. They took a whip made with many strands of leather. Each strand had a sharp bit of metal attached to the end. Then they whipped His back until His skin was bleeding and raw.

Because Jesus is God's Son, He is a king in His Father's kingdom. That's why He is called King of the Jews. (Jesus was Jewish.) The soldiers thought it was funny that this poor, beaten man claimed to be a king, so they made a wreath from some thorny vines and put it on His head.

Then Jesus had to carry a cross made from huge logs all the way out of the city and up a hill. When He reached the top of the hill, the soldiers took long, sharp nails and hammered them through Jesus' hands and feet into the wood of the cross. Then they lifted the cross up and put it in a stand.

Finally, after three hours of unbelievable pain, Jesus died.

To make sure He was dead, the soldiers took a spear and pushed it into Jesus' side. Blood and water poured out of the hole in His side. And Jesus' blood splashed to the ground.

Hold It!

Jesus is just like the lamb that was sacrificed once a year to reconnect people to God.

While Jesus was hanging in pain from the cross, all the sin of all people throughout all time was absorbed into Him. When He died, all the sin that separates people from God was taken away.

When His blood splashed to the earth after He was stabbed, God took some of His blood and sprinkled it on an altar in heaven. His blood covers all the sinful acts that will ever be committed by anyone. When God looks at that altar, all He sees is Jesus' blood.

That's why Jesus has another name that we have not heard yet. Jesus is the "Lamb of God."

Today there is no need for anyone to sacrifice an animal to be reconnected to God. All we need now is to believe and accept that Jesus died so our sin could be taken away. Then we are born again and become citizens of the kingdom of God.

If we make the wrong choices after we are born into God's kingdom, we only need to ask to be forgiven and our sinful actions will be covered with the blood of Jesus.

Because Jesus is the Lamb of God, we can live our lives free from sin and receive forgiveness for our sinful actions. We can be totally connected to God and live our lives as we were meant to—completely alive and filled with all the good things that are ours as citizens of God's eternal kingdom.

Sacrificed

THE GREATEST GIFT

One of the most wonderful parts of the entire Bible is written below. The letters have been scrambled in most of the words. See if you can put the letters in the right order and discover the greatest gift anyone can ever receive.

"roF   God   dovel   het   lorwd   os
chum   tath   He   agev   His   lyon   Son.   God
agev   His   Son   os   tath   whoever   believes   ni   Him
amy   ton   eb   lost   tub   have   eternal   life." (John 3:16)

Unscramble here.

"_ _ _   God   _ _ _ _ _   _ _ _   _ _ _ _ _ _   _ _

_ _ _ _   _ _ _ _   He   _ _ _ _   His   _ _ _ _   Son. God

_ _ _ _   His Son   _ _   _ _ _ _   whoever believes   _ _   Him

_ _ _   _ _ _   _ _   lost   _ _ _   have eternal life." (John 3:16)

Check your answers in the Answer Key at the end of this book

LIVE IT!

THE MOST IMPORTANT THING about a sacrifice is that it is done voluntarily. No one can make you sacrifice anything. They can make you give up something precious to you, but they can't make you want to do it. Sacrifice is actually making the choice to give.

In the days long ago, the people chose to give up the animal for sacrifice to God. Many people who fight wars do it voluntarily—they choose to risk their lives for something they believe in. Parents don't *have* to work. They could refuse to give up their time in order to work and provide for us. But they choose to sacrifice because they love us.

The sacrifice Jesus made when He died on the cross is no different. He actually chose to go through all the pain and all the suffering. He did it because He loves you. He wanted to make sure you could always be connected to God. He wanted to make a way for you to live your life with all the fullness and wonderful things God has for you.

Because of Jesus, it is just like Adam and Eve never sinned.

Remember the story of Adam and Eve? Before Satan convinced them to disobey God, they lived lives that were filled with all the good that God gave them. They had everything they needed. But most of all, they really *knew* God. They talked with Him often and spent time with Him in their garden home. It was like there was a bright, glowing light inside of them that came from being so close to God.

When Adam and Eve chose to disobey God, that wonderful light became dark. The relationship they had with God became distant; they couldn't see Him and talk with Him like before.

But now Jesus has made a way for you to have a relationship with God that is much like the one Adam and Eve enjoyed. You can spend time with Him and actually get to know Him. You can experience the absolute total and unconditional love He has for you. Because of Jesus, the light of really knowing God can be ignited in your own life.

All because Jesus chose to give His life for you.

Sacrificed

GIVE IT

JESUS IS THE PERFECT EXAMPLE of what it means to sacrifice. He gave His life to others while He walked the earth. Then He gave His life so the world could know God.

Sacrifice is difficult to understand, but it is even harder to practice in your own life. Giving up things that are important to us or that we really care about is never easy. But if we want to live like Jesus and follow His example, we need to be willing to give, even when it hurts.

See if you can think of a way to give something to someone else that will really be a sacrifice for you. Maybe you could sacrifice your time and volunteer to look after your brothers or sisters to give your parents a break. Maybe you could sacrifice going somewhere with your friends this weekend and give your time to someone who could use your help.

There are many things you could do. Ask Jesus for ideas. After all, He is the expert.

Jesus gave His life so the world could know God.

WORD GAME

MESSAGE FROM THE *WORD OF PROMISE*

You have learned about Jesus being the "Lamb of God" and what His sacrifice has given you. But death couldn't hold Jesus. For a hint about what's coming in the next chapter, fill in the correct letters in the blanks below to discover a message Jesus gave about Himself. *See if you can figure out the missing letters.*

W	L	M	E	D	P	O	T	B	K
1	2	3	4	5	6	7	8	9	10

S	Y	N	F	H	U	A	R	G	I
11	12	13	14	15	16	17	18	19	20

"_ _ _ _ _ _ _ _ _ _ _ _ _ _ Him _ _ _ _
 8 15 4 12 1 20 2 9 4 17   20 8 15

_ _ _ _ _ _ _ _ _ _ _ _ _ _ kill him.
1 15 20   11 17   5 8 15 4

But _ _ _ _ _ _ _ _ _ _ _ _ _ _ _ _ _ _ _ _ _ _ _ _
      7 13 8 15   8 15   18 5 5 17   17 14   4 18

_ _ _ _ _ _ _ _ _, He _ _ _ _ _ _ _ _ _ _ _
15 11 5 4 17   1   2 2 18   11 4 8

_ _ _ _ _ _ _ _ _ _."
2 20 14   17 19 17 20 13 (Luke 18:33)

Check your answers in the Answer Key at the end of this book

Sacrificed

To prepare for this session, listen to the **WORD OF PROMISE** New Testament recording of:

hear it!

Book of Matthew, chapters 24-26

Book of Mark, chapter 12-13

Book of Luke, chapter 21-22

Jesus' dead body was covered with large strips of soft cloth and buried in a tomb. It was really nothing more than a cave dug in a wall of rock. A large stone was rolled in front to cover the opening.

Jesus' friends were brokenhearted. The One who had taught them for so long was gone; the One they loved had been killed. They were filled with sorrow and confusion. If Jesus had truly been the Son of God, how could He die? If He had all the power and authority of God, how could mere men put Him to death?

Just before Jesus had been put to death, He told His friends that He would rise on the third day. On the day He was buried, soldiers had been sent to guard the tomb. Jesus' enemies were afraid someone would steal Jesus' body to make it look like He had risen from death, so the guards sat near the tomb to watch.

On the third day after Jesus was crucified, a few women who had been his friends went to visit the tomb. They were extremely sad and most likely crying as they walked toward the place where Jesus' body had been laid.

de·fine [it]

CRUCIFIED: This word means to be put to death by being nailed to a cross.

Just as they got to the tomb, the ground beneath their feet began to shake violently. As they struggled to stand, an angel, glowing with brilliant light, came down from heaven. He went straight to the entrance to Jesus' tomb and rolled the stone away. Then he sat on top of the stone.

The guards were so frightened they actually fainted. Their bodies lay on the ground like dead men.

Then the angel spoke to the women who had come to visit Jesus' tomb. He told them that Jesus' body was not there. He told them Jesus had risen from the dead!

GRAB IT!

Since the world began, there have been people who have claimed to have all the right answers. They have tried to convince people they are from God and can teach others how to be reconnected to Him. They may have even told others they are the Messiah.

But God told people long ago how to recognize the true Messiah. The things He said are recorded in the Old Testament part of the Bible.

If you have a Bible with an Old Testament, you can look up what God told them about the Messiah. God said:

de·fine [it]

The **OLD TESTAMENT** consists of the first 39 books in the Bible. Those books tell us the stories about God's people before Jesus was born.

- The Messiah would be born in Bethlehem. (The book of Micah, chapter 5, verse 1—Micah 5:1)
- The Messiah would be born to a woman who had never been with a man. (Isaiah 7:14)
- The Messiah would hear God's voice and teach God's truth. (Deuteronomy 18:18)
- The Messiah would heal people of disease and sickness. (Isaiah 35:5-6)
- The Messiah would be hated even though He was perfect. (Isaiah 53:3)
- The Messiah would be insulted, spat on, and beaten. (Isaiah 50:6)
- The Messiah would be crucified. (Zechariah 12:10)
- The Messiah would rise from the dead. (Isaiah 53:10-11)

Jesus was born in Bethlehem to Mary, a woman who had never been with a man. Because God was His Father, when Jesus lived on earth, He always heard God's voice and taught others the truth about God's kingdom. He acted lovingly toward others at all times. Jesus had the power to make the blind see and the lame walk. He healed people just by touching them and always met the needs of others.

Jesus lived a perfect life, totally without sin. But His enemies hated Him. They had Him beaten by soldiers who insulted Him and spat in His face. Then Jesus was put to death on a cross.

There have been some really good people who have taught things that are true and right. Throughout all the centuries there have been wise people who could under-stand some of God's truth. They may even have done some amazing things. But when those people died, they were buried and never seen again.

When Jesus was put to death, the story was not over, it was only beginning. We can know without doubt that Jesus is the true Messiah because death could not hold Him. Jesus, the Son of God, ROSE AGAIN!

His Life

FIND THE TRUTH

Down

1. Who is the Messiah?
3. What is another name of Jesus that means Messiah?
5. Jesus died for all people. That means _____!
7. Jesus promised He would _____ from death on the third day.
9. If we are born again, we will have new _____ in God's kingdom.
11. This name of Jesus means "rescuer." Jesus rescues us from sin and death.

Across

2. Jesus gave His life as a _____ for you.
4. This word is what a servant does.
6. This is the day we celebrate that Jesus rose from death.
8. To be born again, we must _____ Jesus is God's Son.
10. We should follow Jesus' example and always act loving to _____ people.
12. A special place to worship God is called an _____.

Check your answers in the Answer Key at the end of this book

HOLD IT!

Can you imagine how you would feel if someone you love died? How would you react if someone told you they climbed out of their grave and were alive again?

That's exactly what happened to Jesus' friends.

The women who had seen the angel at the tomb ran to tell everyone that Jesus' body was not there. They told all Jesus' friends what the angel told them—Jesus was alive again!

But Jesus' friends had a hard time believing what the women said. How could a dead man live again? They probably wanted to believe, but dead people just don't get up and leave their graves. Dead means dead, right?

Not long after Jesus came back from death, His friends were together in a room. The door was locked because they were frightened. They feared Jesus' enemies would try to kill them too.

Suddenly, Jesus appeared! He showed His friends the wounds in His hands and feet where the nails had held Him to the cross. They knew beyond a doubt that this was Jesus. And He had risen from death just as He said He would.

But Jesus was different than before He had died. He was able to enter a locked room without a key! Something had changed.

ALIVE AGAIN

The words "alive" and "again" are hidden many times in the grid below. Can you find them all? Remember, the word may be written up, down, backward, forward, or diagonally. (Hint: Both words appear 10 times.)

A	A	E	V	I	L	A	I	E	V	A
A	L	I	V	E	E	G	A	L	G	L
A	I	I	A	L	I	V	E	A	G	I
G	V	E	V	I	L	A	I	A	G	V
A	E	G	L	E	V	N	A	L	I	E
I	N	I	A	G	A	L	V	I	A	E
N	I	A	G	A	L	G	N	V	G	N
I	A	I	A	A	I	A	A	E	A	I
A	G	A	I	N	V	I	L	I	I	A
V	E	L	N	G	E	I	L	V	N	G
A	L	I	V	E	A	G	A	I	N	A

Check your answers in the Answer Key at the end of this book

BEFORE JESUS WAS BORN as a human baby, He had lived with God in heaven. Jesus had complete authority in heaven. Everything He said happened as soon as He spoke the words. Just like God, Jesus had incredible power and authority over everything that was created. Every being in heaven and everything that existed instantly obeyed every word Jesus spoke. That's because Jesus is God.

That can be very confusing and everyone has a hard time trying to understand how Jesus can be the Son of God and also *be* God. But that's only part of understanding God. Actually, God is made up of three different and distinct beings, but there is only one God.

Our God is three beings in one being: Father, Son, and Holy Spirit (we'll learn about Him in the next chapter.)

de•fine [*it*]

HEAVEN: The place where God lives. We know that heaven is above us, but God doesn't live in the sky. God's home is much grander and more beautiful than anything we can imagine.

Think of an egg. It has a shell, a clear part that turns white when you cook it, and the yellow part called a yolk. Each part is different from the other parts, but all together, they make an egg. If you take any of the parts away, there isn't really a whole egg anymore.

Like an egg has three parts, but all of them are an egg, so our God has three beings and all together they are God. This is called the Trinity, meaning "three in one."

Jesus is God, but because Jesus loved people so much, He volunteered to leave heaven and become a man. He willingly took on the limitations of a human being, even though He had total authority over everything as God. He came to earth and lived much as everyone lives, and He died as everyone dies.

But He didn't have to die! He could have simply said, "No" and no one could have hurt Him. Even though He was clothed in human flesh, He was still God.

de•fine [*it*]

RESURRECTION: This word means to be raised from the dead. The day Jesus rose from the dead was His resurrection day. We celebrate His resurrection on Easter.

He died because He chose to die. He died so you could be born again.

And now, Jesus is alive! He took authority over death and rose from His tomb. Because He is alive, you can be absolutely certain that He is exactly who He claimed to be. You can tell everyone: JESUS IS THE MESSIAH!

His Life

GIVE IT

JESUS SPENT MANY DAYS with His friends after He defeated death and came out of His grave. He talked with them and ate with them. In a lot of ways, He seemed the same as before He died. He looked the same and He talked the same; His friends recognized Him easily, but Jesus was very different after He rose from death.

Now Jesus is no longer limited by a human body (His human body died). Jesus has returned to heaven and is a part of the Trinity that is our God.

You can be sure that God knows exactly what it's like to be human. He knows exactly what it feels like to be young. He lived on earth as Jesus. He's been tempted, so He can help you deal with temptation. He's been treated badly, so He knows how to help you learn to forgive.

Before Jesus left His friends and returned to heaven He told them, "You can be sure I will be with you always." But Jesus wasn't just talking to those few people back then. He was talking to you!

Anytime you need Him, He will be there. All you need to do is seek Him.

MESSAGE FROM *THE WORD OF PROMISE*

The words below are written in code. To find the right letters, use the code key. Then put the words in the right order to discover a powerful promise from Jesus. (Hint: one of the words is used twice.)

poaxc = U N T I L   jxcc = __ __ __ __

jxak = __ __ __ __   wq = __ __

jwlct = __ __ __ __ __   nwoaxopb = __ __ __ __ __ __ __ __

fwp = __ __ __   bot = __ __ __

akb = __ __ __

Code Key

A	B	C	D	E	F	G	H	I	J	K	L	M
d	h	n	t	b	q	m	k	x	g	v	c	r

N	O	P	Q	R	S	T	U	V	W	X	Y	Z
o	w	i	e	l	z	a	p	s	j	u	f	y

"I __ __ __ __   __ __ __ __ __ __ __ __ __ __   __ __ T __   __ __ __

__ N __ __ __   __ __ __   __ __ D   __ __   __ __ __   __ __ __ __ __ __."

(Matthew 28:20)

Check your answers in the Answer Key at the end of this book

His Life

To prepare for this session, listen to the *WORD OF PROMISE* New Testament recording of:

Book of Matthew, chapters 27-28

Book of Mark, chapter 14-16

Book of Luke, chapter 23-24

Jesus' friends and followers, called disciples, had watched as Jesus, this Man they loved, was beaten and crucified. They had seen His cold, dead body. They knew Jesus had died. Their hopes and dreams about life with Jesus were crushed. They had thought His death was the end; but now they knew it was really *only the beginning.*

de·fine [*it*]

DISCIPLE: In the Bible, this word means "learner." It is someone who follows another person in order to learn from them.

Jesus had risen from death, just as He said He would! He had returned to the ones who loved Him. He ate with them, talked with them, and spent time being with them. They were amazed, thrilled, filled with awe, joy, and wonder. Nothing could defeat Jesus, not even death.

Jesus' disciples were beginning to understand that Jesus was not just a Man. They began to realize that Jesus is God, so His power is greater than anything or anyone.

They were beginning to understand that the kingdom of God is much more than an earthly place. All earthly kingdoms will one day come to an end, but God's kingdom is eternal. His kingdom is located in heaven, but it is also found in the hearts of those who choose to accept Jesus as Ruler, Messiah, and Lord. (Review the "Get It" section of chapter 1). The people of God's kingdom are those who love God and are born again.

After Jesus rose and appeared to His followers, He stayed with them only a short time. Soon, Jesus knew that it was time for Him to return to His Father in heaven. His time on earth was finished. He had done all God had sent Him to do.

Just before Jesus left, He told His disciples to tell everyone throughout the world that He is the Messiah. He told them to teach everyone all they had learned from Him about God's kingdom. (Jesus wants the entire world to know how to find God's kingdom; He wants everyone to be born again.)

Then, as the disciples watched, Jesus lifted His hands toward heaven. Then, right before their tear-filled eyes, Jesus was lifted up into the clouds, and rose out of their sight!

GRAB IT!

We know that the things Jesus taught will allow us to live successfully in the kingdom of God. We know that Jesus is the only Messiah because He rose from death. We know that we can be born again by believing in Him and accepting Him into our lives. But what does it mean to us that He returned to heaven?

Before Jesus was lifted up into the clouds, He told His disciples that He would be with them forever. Obviously, Jesus didn't mean that He would still live on the earth. He wanted His disciples to know that His love for them would not end. He knew it was important for them to realize that, even after He returned to heaven, He would not forget them. Jesus is still watching over all the people who believe in Him and love Him.

When Jesus returned to heaven, He sat down on His throne. You see, Jesus truly is a King. He is the greatest King—the King of Kings. His throne is in heaven right next to the throne of God.

Because Jesus knows exactly what it is like to live as a man, He knows all about how difficult it can be to live a righteous life. No matter what difficult situation you find yourself in, Jesus knows what you're going through. Because He lived as a man, He suffered all the same things. He was tempted by Satan. He was treated badly and hurt by others. He had people misunderstand Him and lie about Him. Whatever happens in your life, Jesus understands exactly how you feel.

Jesus is now in heaven with God. He loves you and cares deeply about everything that happens to you. He knows exactly what you need at all times. So Jesus talks to God about you. He asks God to send you whatever you need as you learn to live in His kingdom. Jesus actually prays for you!

For You

WORDS OF LIFE

Below you will find 12 words that you have learned in this study. See if you can match the word to the correct definition.

ANOINTED

Something with no beginning and no end; it will never change and will last forever.

OBEDIENCE

To voluntarily give something precious away.

ETERNAL

Set apart or chosen for special service to God.

PARABLE

People who believe that Jesus is the Messiah and have received new, eternal life from Him.

GLORY

A special structure of some sort set aside for worshipping God.

RIGHTEOUSNESS

The place where God lives.

CHRISTIAN

Killed by being nailed to a cross.

SACRIFICE

To listen closely with respect and be willing to follow instructions.

ALTAR

To be raised from death.

CRUCIFIED

A short story about something familiar to help explain things that are hard to understand.

HEAVEN

The ability Jesus gives us to live our lives in the way that pleases God.

RESURRECTION

Honor, respect, and love given to God.

Check your answers in the Answer Key at the end of this book

HOLD IT!

One of the last promises Jesus gave His disciples before He returned to heaven was that He would send them help to live their lives as God wants. That Helper is the Holy Spirit.

The Holy Spirit is one of the three persons of the Trinity. The Holy Spirit is God, so He has all the same power and authority as God the Father and God the Son (Jesus).

Although the Holy Spirit has always existed and always helped people understand God's kingdom, He did not always live *with* people. In the Old Testament, the Holy Spirit acted in the lives of people when they needed His help, but He did not actually live with them. Because Jesus has now sent the Holy Spirit to us, the Holy Spirit lives with Christians constantly. He is so close that, if you try, you can even feel His presence.

Whenever we are confused about living our lives in the right way, the Holy Spirit will help us understand. If we need help making right choices, the Holy Spirit will lead us to do the right thing. He will cause us to be able to understand the truth of the Bible and learn more about life in God's kingdom. The Holy Spirit is present with us at all times and, if we are willing to accept His help, He will bring us power to live righteous lives that please God.

The Holy Spirit will also help us obey Jesus' words, "tell people to change their hearts and lives."

Just before Jesus rose to heaven, He told His disciples to tell the whole world about Him. Jesus knew that His disciples needed help to be able to tell others about Him. He knew they were concerned that others would not believe them, and might even laugh at them. And Jesus was aware that His disciples still had much to learn about God's kingdom. So Jesus told His followers to wait until the Holy Spirit came to them.

When the Holy Spirit lives in the lives of people, He causes them to be bold and brave in God's kingdom. The Holy Spirit helps people to know what is right in God's eyes and helps them avoid sinful attitudes and actions. He helps believers know when it is right to speak and what to say.

Without the Holy Spirit, we would not have the ability to really help others believe that Jesus is the Messiah.

HIDDEN MESSAGE

Each session in this book has a title. In the spaces below, copy the title of each session in the order it appears. You will find a hidden message about Jesus.

_____ ___ ___ _____ ____ ____ ____

_____ _____ _____ _____. _____ _____

_____ ____ ____ ____ ____ ____ _____

___ ____ ____ ____. ____ _____

_____ ___ ____ ___ ___.

Check your answers in the Answer Key at the end of this book

Who is Jesus?

LIVE IT!

BEFORE JESUS WAS CRUCIFIED, He gave His disciples an incredible promise. He told them that one day He would return.

Some day in the future (no one knows when) Jesus will appear in the clouds above the earth. Then, as quickly as you can blink your eye, everyone who has been born again—those who are alive and those whose bodies have died—will suddenly be lifted up into the air to meet Him.

Can you even imagine how fabulous that will be? How wonderful to actually see Jesus!

After we all meet Him in the air, He will take us to heaven, God's heavenly kingdom, to live with Him forever.

Heaven is more beautiful than anything you have ever seen. It is filled with light, but there is no sun—no glaring heat. All the light in God's kingdom comes from Jesus, the light of the world. God's heavenly kingdom is golden and filled with precious things.

In God's heavenly kingdom there is no sickness, no death, no suffering of any kind. It is filled with joy beyond your wildest dreams and never-ending peace. Love is everywhere, in everything. Everything is perfect. Everything is eternal.

Jesus said He was going to prepare a place in heaven for us to live. If you are a part of God's kingdom, Jesus has created a special place for you. It is a place that is more beautiful and more wonderful than anything you can imagine. It is an ideal place where you can live in perfect peace, love, and joy forever with Jesus.

Jesus said He would rise again, and He did. He also told us He will return from heaven and take all God's people to live with Him there. You can be certain Jesus will do exactly as He said. He will come again!

GIVE IT

IF YOU ARE A CHRISTIAN, you have the Holy Spirit in your life. Jesus sent the Holy Spirit to you so that you can live your life as Jesus lived His. The Holy Spirit will always lead you to choose the things that please God.

When you allow the Holy Spirit to lead you and help you live your life in the right way, people will see that you are different. They will wonder why you seem to understand things better and make better choices. They will begin to realize that your attitude is positive and you treat others with love, consideration, and respect.

Living your life in the ways that please God is the best way for you to tell people about Jesus. They will be able to see exactly what Jesus is like by looking at your life. They will know you have something in your life that is missing in theirs, and they will wonder why. You will be able to tell them: it's not a question of why, it's all about Jesus—it's all about Who.

Jesus told His disciples to go to the whole world and tell others about Him and how they can be born into God's kingdom. This is called "The Great Commission." If you believe Jesus is the Messiah and you are born again, then you are one of His disciples. So Jesus wants you to tell everyone about Him.

When others see your life and ask you why it's different from theirs, the Holy Spirit will help you find the right words to tell them about Jesus and God's kingdom. Then you can help them be born again.

There is nothing you could ever do for anyone that is so important. There is no gift as precious as new life in God's kingdom. When you share with others what Jesus has done for you, you help them find new, eternal life.

So do as Jesus told all His disciples to do: Go and tell all the world Jesus is the one and only Messiah. And He came to save the world.

MESSAGE FROM THE *WORD OF PROMISE*

Did you know that in the prayer that Jesus prayed just before He was crucified, He prayed for you? Part of that prayer is in code below. The alphabet has been scrambled and each letter actually stands for another letter (for example: A=g and S=y). *To break the code try to discover the letter that should have been used.* Some letters have been decoded for you. Hint: As you discover the right letter, write it into the grid.

A	B	C	D	E	F	G	H	I	J	K	L	M
	q	t	j					u	a	w		h

N	O	P	Q	R	S	T	U	V	W	X	Y	Z
c		l	v	y					m	s		x

"F A T H E R, _ _ _ _ _ _ _ _ _ _ _ _ _ _ _ L _
 n g d k o b u m g c d d k o y o l o e l f o

_ _ _ _ Y O U _ _ _ G _ _ _ _ _ _ _ _ _ _
d k g d p e i k g z o r u z o c h o d e q o

_ _ _ _ _ _ _ _ E V E R Y _ _ _ _ _ _ I _ _."
m u d k h o u c o z o b p l f g t o u g h

(John 17:24)

Check your answers in the Answer Key at the end of this book.

Jesus became a man and spent His life teaching about the kingdom of God **FOR YOU**.

Jesus gave His life as a ransom **FOR YOU.**

Jesus rose from death and is now with His Father in heaven where He prays **FOR YOU.**

One day Jesus will return to take all those who are in God's kingdom to be with Him forever. Is He coming back **FOR YOU**?

For You

journaling **WHO Is Jesus:**

journaling WHO Is Jesus:

journaling WHO Is Jesus:

WHO Is Jesus:

journaling WHO Is Jesus:

journaling WHO Is Jesus:

journaling WHO Is Jesus:

journaling WHO Is Jesus:

journaling **WHO Is Jesus:**

_____

_____

_____

_____

_____

_____

_____

_____

_____

_____

_____

_____

_____

_____

_____

_____

_____

_____

_____

_____

_____

journaling **WHO Is Jesus:**

_____

_____

_____

_____

_____

_____

_____

_____

_____

_____

_____

_____

_____

_____

_____

_____

_____

_____

_____

WHO Is Jesus:

journaling WHO Is Jesus:

_____

_____

_____

_____

_____

_____

_____

_____

_____

_____

_____

_____

_____

_____

_____

_____

_____

_____

_____

_____

_____

journaling WHO Is Jesus:

WHO Is Jesus:

_____

_____

_____

_____

_____

_____

_____

_____

_____

_____

_____

_____

_____

_____

_____

_____

_____

_____

_____

_____

_____

_____

_____

_____

journaling WHO Is Jesus:

journaling WHO Is Jesus:

journaling **WHO Is Jesus:**

_____

_____

_____

_____

_____

_____

_____

_____

_____

_____

_____

_____

_____

_____

_____

_____

_____

_____

_____

_____

_____

_____

_____

journaling WHO Is Jesus:

journaling WHO Is Jesus:

journaling WHO Is Jesus:

journaling WHO Is Jesus:

journaling **WHO Is Jesus:**

journaling **WHO Is Jesus:**

journaling **WHO Is Jesus:**

journaling WHO Is Jesus:

journaling WHO Is Jesus:

journaling WHO Is Jesus:

journaling WHO Is Jesus:

journaling **WHO Is Jesus:**

journaling WHO Is Jesus:

journaling WHO Is Jesus:

journaling WHO Is Jesus:

WHO Is Jesus:

journaling WHO Is Jesus:

journaling **WHO Is Jesus:**

_____

_____

_____

_____

_____

_____

_____

_____

_____

_____

_____

_____

_____

_____

_____

_____

_____

_____

_____

_____

_____

_____

journaling WHO Is Jesus:

journaling **WHO Is Jesus:**

ANSWER KEY

Answer to Name Game on Page 4

```
D G O L O R E T S A M T H E E V
E S Z B M A R T E A C H E R Q R
L O S N A M J K C R H E I E B O
I N P U L T E H M X R T Z D R L
V O W V F M X S K H I R S E O E
E F N L C P J E S U S U O E I S
R G D O R D M Z W I T T R M V N
E O O L T H E W A Y A H W E A U
R D R O L O R M Y X P H Z R S O
V X U I Q B H O L Y O N E V A C
I W P R I N C E O F P E A C E I
L O A S W E J E H T F O G N I K
E F G P I M M A N U E L D G O L
D A S H E P H E R D L M B Q R S
U Z S O N O F M A N P W Z R L N
B X V R T O L L U F R E D N O W
```

Answer to *Connect the Name* Name Game on Page 8

```
G
F
C
B
A
D
H
E
```

Answer to *Message from the Word of Promise* Word Game on Page 10

"I came to give life—life in all its fullness." (John 10:10)

Answer to *Find the Prophecy* Word Game on Page 12

ISAIAH 40:3, 4, 5

This is the voice of a man who calls out:
"Prepare in the desert the way of the Lord.
Make the road in the dry lands straight for our God.
Every valley should be raised up.
Every mountain and hill should be made flat.
The rough ground should be made level.
The rugged ground should be made smooth.
Then the glory of the Lord will be shown.
All people together will see it.
The Lord himself said these things."

Answer to *Discover the New Testament* Word Game on Page 14

Matthew, Mark, Luke, John, Acts, Romans, 1 Corinthians, 2 Corinthians, Galatians, Ephesians, Philippians, Colossians, 1 Thessalonians, 2 Thessalonians, 1 Timothy, 2 Timothy, Titus, Philemon, Hebrews, James, 1 Peter, 2 Peter, 1 John, 2 John, 3 John, Jude, Revelation

Answer to *Message from the Word of Promise* Word Game on Page 17

My mother and my brothers are those who listen to God's teaching and obey it!
Luke 8:21

Answer to *What's the Attitude?* Word Game on Page 19

REBELLIOUS   OBEDIENT
ANGRY   HUMBLE
UNCARING   LOVING
PROUD   FRIENDLY
SELFISH   HELPFUL

ANSWER KEY

Answer to *Find the Promise* Word Game on Page 21

Those who want to do right more than anything else are happy. God will fully satisfy them. (Matthew 5:6)

Answer to *Message from the Word of Promise* Word Game on Page 23

...you should be a light for other people. Live so that they will see the good things you do. (Matthew 5:16)

Answer to *Find the Right Path* Maze on Page 25

Answer to *It's in There* Word Game on Page 28

sin, for, gives, forgives, given, forgiven, never, ever , even, give

Answer to *Message from the Word of Promise* Word Game on Page 30

"...Forgive other people and you will be forgiven." (Luke 6:37)

Answer to *The Giving List* Word Game on Page 32

Care, Time, Food, Help, Gifts, Hope, Joy, Peace, Prayer

Answer to *Samaritan Search* Word Game on Page 34

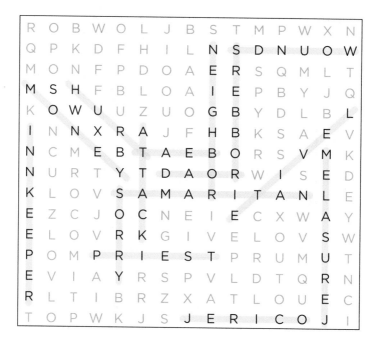

Answer to *Message from the Word of Promise* Word Game on Page 36

"...You must love your neighbor as yourself." (Luke 10:27)

Answer to *What Will Grow?* Word Game on Page 39

Responsibility – Reliability

Happiness – Cheerfulness

Truthfulness – Honesty

Joy – Delight

Peace – Harmony

Anger – Rage

Selfishness – Self-centeredness

Dishonesty – Lying

Negative thinking – Gloominess

Positive thinking – Hopefulness

Answer to *Message from the Word of Promise* Word Game on Page 43

"...But what is the seed that fell on the good ground? That seed is like the person who hears the teaching and understands it." (Matthew 13:23)

Answer to *Words of Love* Word Game on Page 46

Answer to *Find Success* Word Game on Page 48

ANSWER KEY

Answer to *Message from the Word of Promise* Word Game on Page 50

"The thing you should want most is God's kingdom and doing what God wants." (Matthew 6:33)

Answer to *Following Directions* Word Game on Page 53

Little children are humble and willing to learn.

Answer to *Message from the Word of Promise* Word Game on Page 58

"The greatest person in the kingdom of heaven is the one who makes himself humble like this child." (Matthew 18:4)

Answer to *Return to God's Kingdom* Maze on Page 61

ANSWER KEY

Answer to *Message from the Word of Promise* Word Game on Page 64

"The Son of Man came to give his life to save many people." (Matthew 20:28)

Answer to *Holidays* Word Game on Page 66

1. Christmas
2. Easter
3. Thanksgiving
4. Valentine's Day
5. Pentecost
6. Memorial Day
7. Labor Day

Answer to *The Greatest Gift* Word Game on Page 70

"For God loved the world so much that He gave His only Son. God gave His Son so that whoever believes in Him may not be lost, but have eternal life." (John 3:16)

Answer to *Message from the Word of Promise* Word Game on Page 73

"They will beat Him with whips and then kill him. But on the third day after His death, he will rise to life again." (Luke 18:33)